the
poetry
of
John
Donne

ISBN
9781788885188

the
poetry
of
John
Donne

This edition published in 2019 by Arcturus Publishing Limited
26/27 Bickels Yard, 151–153 Bermondsey Street,
London SE1 3HA

AD006514UK

Printed in the UK

MIX
Paper from
responsible sources
FSC® C018072

Contents

Section II: Elegies

Section III: Epithalamia (Marriage Songs)

Section IV: Satires

Section V: Verse Letters

Section VI: Divine Poems

Introduction

A contemporary of Shakespeare, John Donne was one of a group of poets described by Samuel Johnson as the 'Metaphysical' school. Their work was characterized by philosophical exploration, irony, clever conceits, an informality of linguistic style and a flexibility of metre. Donne's poems focus largely on love, religion and morality. The directness of his language and the close reasoning of his arguments, together with the absence of long, descriptive passages, marked a striking departure from the more conventional writings of his time.

John Donne was born in London in 1572 into a wealthy Catholic family during a time of severe anti-Catholicism in England. His mother was the grand-niece of the Catholic martyr Sir Thomas More, and his father, also called John, died when his son was four. Religion would become increasingly important to Donne, although his faith would be tested by events throughout his life.

Donne was a diligent student who studied at both Oxford (where he began his studies aged 11) and Cambridge universities. But despite his hard work he was not awarded a degree because, as a Catholic, he could not bring himself to swear the required oath of allegiance to the Protestant Queen Elizabeth I. Donne travelled abroad during the early 1590s, probably in Spain and Italy, allegedly frittering away his considerable inheritance on women and 'other pastimes'. He wrote many of his love lyrics during these years; they were collected in manuscript form as *Satires* and *Songs and Sonnets*, and many of them are included in this collection.

In 1593, Donne's brother Henry was arrested for

harbouring a Catholic priest; he was imprisoned and he died in Newgate after contracting the bubonic plague. Henry's fate appears to have prompted Donne's eventual conversion from Catholicism to Anglicanism.

On his return from the continent, Donne studied law at Thavies Inn and Lincoln's Inn in London. He then enlisted to serve in the naval battles of the Anglo-Spanish War, sailing with Sir Walter Raleigh and the Earl of Essex in buccaneering expeditions to the Azores. Returning to England once more, Donne was appointed private secretary to Sir Thomas Egerton, Lord Keeper of the Great Seal, serving him for five years and living as a member of his household on the Strand. A few years later Donne became a member of Parliament.

While living at the Strand, Donne met and fell in love with Anne More – the daughter of Sir George More and niece (by marriage) of Egerton's wife. Certain that there would be no chance of obtaining Sir George's blessing on their union (Anne was only 17 and Donne was nearly 30), the couple married in secret. Sir George was furious: he dismissed Donne from his post and had him thrown into prison. Donne's career in public service was at an end. Anne's father also denied his daughter a dowry. Contemplating their future of poverty, Donne wrote a letter to his wife which closed with the words, 'John Donne, Anne Donne, Undone.'

During the next ten years, Donne was unable to find work and he and Anne lived in penury. With his family expanding rapidly (Anne bore twelve children, five of whom died before they reached adulthood), Donne continued to study and write, publishing the *Divine Poems* (many of which are included here) in 1607. In 1610, he wrote *Pseudo-Martyr*, a renunciation of his faith in which he argued that Catholics could support King James I without compromising their beliefs. In return, Donne was appointed a royal chaplain. But this improvement in his professional life was accompanied by personal grief. Two years after his ordination, in 1617, Anne died, aged 33, after giving birth to a stillborn baby.

In 1621, Donne became Dean of St Paul's Cathedral and then vicar of St Dunstan-in-the-West in Fleet Street, where he earned a reputation as one of the foremost preachers of his day. By this point, his poetry and other writings were no longer concerned with the love of women but with religious devotion. His *Holy Sonnets*, also represented here, focus on the complex relationship between man and God. In 1624, Donne fell seriously ill and, although continuing to preach in front of huge crowds, became obsessed with death. He died of stomach cancer in February 1631, with few published poems to his name. Today, he is considered by many to be the finest love poet in the English language.

SECTION I:
SONGS AND SONNETS

Air and Angels

Twice or thrice had I lov'd thee,
Before I knew thy face or name;
So in a voice, so in a shapeless flame
Angels affect us oft, and worshipp'd be;
    Still when, to where thou wert, I came,
Some lovely glorious nothing I did see.
But since my soul, whose child love is,
Takes limbs of flesh, and else could nothing do,
More subtle than the parent is
Love must not be, but take a body too,
And therefore what thou wert, and who
I bid Love ask, and now
That it assume thy body, I allow,
And fix itself in thy lip, eye, and brow.

Whilst thus to ballast love, I thought,
And so more steadily to have gone,
With wares which would sink admiration,
I saw I had love's pinnace overfraught;
Ev'ry thy hair for love to work upon
Is much too much, some fitter must be sought;
For, nor in nothing, nor in things
Extreme, and scatt'ring bright, can love inhere;
Then, as an angel, face, and wings
Of air, not pure as it, yet pure doth wear,
So thy love may be my love's sphere;
    Just such disparity
As is 'twixt air and angels' purity,
'Twixt women's love, and men's, will ever be.

The Anniversary

All kings, and all their favourites,
All glory of honours, beauties, wits,
The sun itself, which makes times, as they pass,
Is elder by a year now than it was
When thou and I first one another saw:
All other things to their destruction draw,
  Only our love hath no decay;
This no tomorrow hath, nor yesterday,
Running it never runs from us away,
  But truly keeps his first, last, everlasting day.

Two graves must hide thine and my corse;
  If one might, death were no divorce,
Alas, as well as other princes, we
(Who prince enough in one another be)
Must leave at last in death these eyes and ears,
Oft fed with true oaths, and with sweet salt tears;
  But souls where nothing dwells but love
(All other thoughts being inmates) then shall prove
This, or a love increased there above,
  When bodies to their graves, souls from their graves
    remove.

And then we shall be throughly blessed;
  But we no more than all the rest.
Here upon earth we are kings, and none but we
Can be such kings, nor of such subjects be;
Who is so safe as we? where none can do
Treason to us, except one of us two.
  True and false fears let us refrain,

Let us love nobly, and live, and add again
Years and years unto years, till we attain
   To write threescore: this is the second of our reign.

The Apparition

When by thy scorn, O murd'ress, I am dead
And that thou think'st thee free
From all solicitation from me,
Then shall my ghost come to thy bed,
And thee, feign'd vestal, in worse arms shall see:
Then thy sick taper will begin to wink,
And he, whose thou art then, being tir'd before,
Will, if thou stir, or pinch to wake him, think
     Thou call'st for more,
And, in false sleep, will from thee shrink:
And then, poor aspen wretch, neglected thou
Bathed in a cold quicksilver sweat wilt lie
     A verier ghost than I.
What I will say, I will not tell thee now,
Lest that preserve thee; and since my love is spent,
I'd rather thou shouldst painfully repent,
Than by my threatenings rest still innocent.

The Bait

Come live with me, and be my love,
And we will some new pleasures prove
Of golden sands, and crystal brooks,
With silken lines, and silver hooks.

There will the river whispering run
Warm'd by thy eyes, more than the sun.
And there the' enamour'd fish will stay,
Begging themselves they may betray.

When thou wilt swim in that live bath,
Each fish, which every channel hath,
Will amorously to thee swim,
Gladder to catch thee, than thou him.

If thou, to be so seen, be'est loth,
By sun, or moon, thou darkenest both,
And if myself have leave to see,
I need not their light, having thee.

Let others freeze with angling reeds,
And cut their legs with shells and weeds,
Or treacherously poor fish beset,
With strangling snare, or windowy net:

Let coarse bold hands from slimy nest
The bedded fish in banks out-wrest,
Or curious traitors, sleeve-silk flies
Bewitch poor fishes' wandering eyes.

For thee, thou need'st no such deceit,
For thou thyself art thine own bait;
That fish, that is not catch'd thereby,
Alas, is wiser far than I.

The Blossom

Little think'st thou, poor flower,
  Whom I have watch'd six or seven days,
And seen thy birth, and seen what every hour
Gave to thy growth, thee to this height to raise,
And now dost laugh and triumph on this bough,
      Little think'st thou
That it will freeze anon, and that I shall
Tomorrow find thee fallen, or not at all.

Little think'st thou, poor heart,
  That labourest yet to nestle thee,
And think'st by hovering here to get a part
In a forbidden or forbidding tree,
And hop'st her stiffness by long siege to bow,
      Little think'st thou
That thou tomorrow, ere the sun doth wake,
Must with the sun and me a journey take.

But thou, which lov'st to be
  Subtle to plague thyself, wilt say,
Alas, if you must go, what's that to me?
Here lies my business, and here I will stay:
You go to friends, whose love and means present
      Various content
To your eyes, ears, and taste, and every part;
If then your body go, what need you a heart?

Well then, stay here; but know
  When thou hast stay'd and done thy most,
A naked thinking heart that makes no show

Is to a woman but a kind of ghost.
How shall she know my heart; or having none,
        Know thee for one?
Practice may make her know some other part;
But take my word, she doth not know a heart.

  Meet me at London, then,
    Twenty days hence, and thou shalt see
Me fresher and more fat, by being with men,
Than if I had stay'd still with her and thee.
For God's sake, if you can, be you so too;
        I will give you
There to another friend, whom we shall find
As glad to have my body as my mind.

Break of Day

'Tis true, 'tis day; what though it be?
O wilt thou therefore rise from me?
Why should we rise, because 'tis light?
Did we lie down because 'twas night?
Love, which in spite of darkness brought us hither,
Should in despite of light keep us together.

Light hath no tongue, but is all eye;
If it could speak as well as spy,
This were the worst that it could say,
That being well, I fain would stay,
And that I loved my heart and honour so
That I would not from him, that had them, go.

Must business thee from hence remove?
O, that's the worst disease of love,
The poor, the foul, the false, love can
Admit, but not the busied man.
He which hath business, and makes love, doth do
Such wrong, as when a married man doth woo.

The Broken Heart

He is stark mad, whoever says
  That he hath been in love an hour,
Yet not that love so soon decays,
  But that it can ten in less space devour;
Who will believe me if I swear
That I have had the plague a year?
  Who would not laugh at me if I should say
  I saw a flash of powder burn a day?

Ah, what a trifle is a heart,
  If once into love's hands it come!
All other griefs allow a part
  To other griefs, and ask themselves but some;
They come to us, but us love draws;
He swallows us and never chaws;
  By him, as by chain-shot, whole ranks do die;
  He is the tyrant pike, our hearts the fry.

If 'twere not so, what did become
  Of my heart when I first saw thee?
I brought a heart into the room,
  But from the room I carried none with me.
If it had gone to thee, I know
Mine would have taught thine heart to show
  More pity unto me; but love, alas,
  At one first blow did shiver it as glass.

Yet nothing can to nothing fall,
  Nor any place be empty quite;
Therefore I think my breast hath all

Those pieces still, though they be not unite;
And now, as broken glasses show
A hundred lesser faces, so
   My rags of heart can like, wish, and adore,
   But after one such love, can love no more.

The Canonization

For God's sake hold your tongue, and let me love,
Or chide my palsy, or my gout,
My five grey hairs, or ruined fortune flout,
With wealth your state, your mind with arts improve,
   Take you a course, get you a place,
    Observe his honour, or his grace,
Or the king's real, or his stamped face
Contemplate; what you will, approve,
So you will let me love.

Alas, alas, who's injured by my love?
What merchant's ships have my sighs drowned?
Who says my tears have overflowed his ground?
When did my colds a forward spring remove?
   When did the heats which my veins fill
    Add one more to the plaguy bill?
Soldiers find wars, and lawyers find out still
Litigious men, which quarrels move,
Though she and I do love.

Call us what you will, we are made such by love;
Call her one, me another fly,
We're tapers too, and at our own cost die,
And we in us find the eagle and the dove.
   The phoenix riddle hath more wit
    By us; we two being one, are it.
So, to one neutral thing both sexes fit.
We die and rise the same, and prove
Mysterious by this love.

We can die by it, if not live by love,
And if unfit for tombs and hearse
Our legend be, it will be fit for verse;
And if no piece of chronicle we prove,
    We'll build in sonnets pretty rooms;
    As well a well-wrought urn becomes
The greatest ashes, as half-acre tombs,
And by these hymns, all shall approve
Us canonized for Love.

And thus invoke us: 'You, whom reverend love
Made one another's hermitage;
You, to whom love was peace, that now is rage;
Who did the whole world's soul contract, and drove
    Into the glasses of your eyes
    (So made such mirrors, and such spies,
That they did all to you epitomize)
Countries, towns, courts: beg from above
A pattern of your love!'

Community

Good we must love and must hate ill,
For ill is ill, and good good still;
  But there are things indifferent,
Which we may neither hate nor love,
But one and then another prove,
  As we shall find our fancy bent.

If then at first wise Nature had
Made women either good or bad,
  Then some we might hate and some choose;
But since she did them so create,
That we may neither love nor hate,
  Only this rests, all, all may use.

If they were good it would be seen;
Good is as visible as green,
  And to all eyes itself betrays.
If they were bad, they could not last;
Bad doth itself and others waste;
  So they deserve nor blame, nor praise.

But they are ours as fruits are ours;
He that but tastes, he that devours,
  And he that leaves all, doth as well;
Changed loves are but changed sorts of meat;
And when he hath the kernel eat,
  Who doth not fling away the shell?

The Computation

For the first twenty years, since yesterday,
I scarce believ'd thou could'st be gone away,
For forty more, I fed on favours past,
And forty on hopes, that thou would'st, they might last.
Tears drown'd one hundred, and sighs blew out two,
A thousand, I did neither think nor do,
Or not divide, all being one thought of you;
Or in a thousand more, forgot that too.
Yet call not this long life; but think that I
Am, by being dead, immortal; can ghosts die?

Confined Love

Some man unworthy to be possessor
Of old or new love, himself being false or weak,
  Thought his pain and shame would be lesser
If on womankind he might his anger wreak;
          And thence a law did grow,
          One might but one man know;
          But are other creatures so?

  Are sun, moon, or stars by law forbidden
To smile where they list, or lend away their light?
  Are birds divorced or are they chidden
If they leave their mate, or lie abroad a-night?
          Beasts do no jointures lose
          Though they new lovers choose;
          But we are made worse than those.

  Who e'er rigg'd fair ships to lie in harbours,
And not to seek lands, or not to deal withal?
  Or built fair houses, set trees, and arbours,
Only to lock up, or else to let them fall?
          Good is not good unless
          A thousand it possess,
          But doth waste with greediness.

The Curse

Whoever guesses, thinks, or dreams he knows
Who is my mistress, wither by this curse;
        Him, only for his purse,
        May some dull whore to love dispose
And then yield unto all that are his foes;
  May he be scorn'd by one, whom all else scorn,
  Forswear to others what to her he hath sworn,
  With fear of missing, shame of getting, torn.

Madness his sorrow, gout his cramps may he
Make, by but thinking who hath made them such;
        And may he feel no touch
        Of conscience, but of fame, and be
Anguish'd, not that 'twas sin, but that 'twas she;
  Or may he for her virtue reverence
  One that hates him only for impotence,
  And equal traitors be she and his sense.

May he dream treason, and believe that he
Meant to perform it, and confess, and die,
        And no record tell why;
        His sons, which none of his may be,
Inherit nothing but his infamy;
  Or may he so long parasites have fed,
  That he would fain be theirs whom he hath bred,
  And at the last be circumcised for bread.

The venom of all stepdames, gamesters' gall,
What tyrants and their subjects interwish,
        What plants, mines, beasts, fowl, fish,

Can contribute, all ill, which all
Prophets or poets spake, and all which shall
Be annex'd in schedules unto this by me,
Fall on that man; for if it be a she,
Nature beforehand hath out-cursèd me.

The Damp

When I am dead, and doctors know not why,
        And my friends' curiosity
Will have me cut up to survey each part,
When they shall find your picture in my heart,
        You think a sudden damp of love
        Will through all their senses move,
And work on them as me, and so prefer
Your murder to the name of massacre.

Poor victories; but if you dare be brave
        And pleasure in your conquest have,
First kill th' enormous giant, your Disdain;
And let th' enchantress Honour next be slain;
        And like a Goth and Vandal rise,
        Deface records and histories
Of your own arts and triumphs over men,
And without such advantage kill me then.

For I could muster up, as well as you,
        My giants and my witches, too,
Which are vast Constancy and Secretness;
But these I neither look for nor profess;
        Kill me as woman, let me die
        As a mere man; do you but try
Your passive valour, and you shall find then,
Naked you have odds enough of any man.

The Dissolution

She's dead; and all which die
    To their first elements resolve;
And we were mutual elements to us,
    And made of one another.
  My body then doth hers involve,
And those things whereof I consist, hereby
In me abundant grow, and burdenous,
    And nourish not, but smother.
  My fire of passion, sighs of air,
Water of tears, and earthly sad despair,
    Which my materials be,
But near worn out by love's security,
She, to my loss, doth by her death repair,
    And I might live long wretched so,
But that my fire doth with my fuel grow.
    Now, as those active kings
  Whose foreign conquest treasure brings,
Receive more, and spend more, and soonest break:
This – which I am amazed that I can speak –
  This death, hath with my store
    My use increased.
And so my soul, more earnestly released,
Will outstrip hers; as bullets flown before
A latter bullet may o'ertake, the powder being more.

The Dream

Dear love, for nothing less than thee
Would I have broke this happy dream;
       It was a theme
For reason, much too strong for fantasy.
Therefore thou waked'st me wisely; yet
My dream thou brokest not, but continued'st it.
Thou art so true, that thoughts of thee suffice
To make dreams truths, and fables histories;
Enter these arms, for since thou thought'st it best,
Not to dream all my dream, let's act the rest.

As lightning, or a taper's light,
Thine eyes, and not thy noise waked me;
       Yet I thought thee
(For thou lov'st truth) an angel, at first sight;
But when I saw thou saw'st my heart,
And knew'st my thoughts beyond an angel's art,
When thou knew'st what I dreamt, when thou knew'st
  when
Excess of joy would wake me, and camest then,
I must confess, it could not choose but be
Profane, to think thee anything but thee.

Coming and staying show'd thee, thee,
But rising makes me doubt, that now
       Thou art not thou.
That love is weak where fear's as strong as he;
'Tis not all spirit, pure and brave,
If mixture it of fear, shame, honour, have;
Perchance as torches, which must ready be,

Men light and put out, so thou deal'st with me;
Thou cam'st to kindle, go'st to come; then I
Will dream that hope again, but else would die.

The Ecstasy

Where, like a pillow on a bed,
A pregnant bank swell'd up to rest
The violet's reclining head,
Sat we two, one another's best.

Our hands were firmly cemented
With a fast balm, which thence did spring;
Our eye-beams twisted, and did thread
Our eyes upon one double string;

So to intergraft our hands, as yet
Was all our means to make us one,
And pictures in our eyes to get
Was all our propagation.

As 'twixt two equal armies, fate
Suspends uncertain victory,
Our souls (which to advance their state,
Were gone out) hung 'twixt her and me.

And whilst our souls negotiate there,
We like sepulchral statues lay;
All day, the same our postures were,
And we said nothing, all the day.

If any, so by love refin'd
That he soul's language understood,
And by good love were grown all mind,
Within convenient distance stood,

He (though he knew not which soul spake,
Because both meant, both spake the same)
Might thence a new concoction take,
And part far purer than he came.

This ecstasy doth unperplex,
We said, and tell us what we love;
We see by this it was not sex,
We see, we saw not what did move;

But as all several souls contain
Mixture of things, they know not what,
Love these mixed souls doth mix again
And makes both one, each this and that.

A single violet transplant,
The strength, the colour, and the size,
(All which before was poor and scant)
Redoubles still, and multiplies.

When love with one another so
Interinanimates two souls,
That abler soul, which thence doth flow,
Defects of loneliness controls.

We then, who are this new soul, know
Of what we are compos'd and made,
For th' atomies of which we grow
Are souls, whom no change can invade.

But O alas, so long, so far,
Our bodies why do we forbear?

They are ours, though they're not we; we are
The intelligences, they the spheres.

We owe them thanks, because they thus
Did us, to us, at first convey,
Yielded their senses' force to us,
Nor are dross to us, but allay.

On man heaven's influence works not so,
But that it first imprints the air;
So soul into the soul may flow,
Though it to body first repair.

As our blood labours to beget
Spirits, as like souls as it can,
Because such fingers need to knit
That subtle knot which makes us man:

So must pure lovers' souls descend
T'affections and to faculties,
Which sense may reach and apprehend,
Else a great prince in prison lies.

To our bodies turn we then, that so
Weak men on love revealed may look;
Love's mysteries in souls do grow,
But yet the body is his book.

And if some lover, such as we,
Have heard this dialogue of one,
Let him still mark us, he shall see
Small change, when we'are to bodies gone.

The Extirpation

So, so, break off this last lamenting kiss,
   Which sucks two souls, and vapours both away;
Turn, thou ghost, that way, and let me turn this,
   And let ourselves benight our happiest day.
We ask none leave to love; nor will we owe
   Any so cheap a death as saying, 'Go;'

'Go;' and if that word have not quite killed thee,
   Ease me with death, by bidding me go too.
Or, if it have, let my word work on me,
   And a just office on a murderer do.
Except it be too late, to kill me so,
   Being double dead, going, and bidding, 'Go.'

Farewell to Love

      Whilst yet to prove
I thought there was some deity in love,
   So did I reverence, and gave
Worship ; as atheists at their dying hour
Call, what they cannot name, an unknown power,
     As ignorantly did I crave.
       Thus when
Things not yet known are coveted by men,
   Our desires give them fashion, and so
As they wax lesser, fall, as they size, grow.

     But, from late fair,
His highness sitting in a golden chair,
   Is not less cared for after three days
By children, than the thing which lovers so
Blindly admire, and with such worship woo;
   Being had, enjoying it decays ;
       And thence,
What before pleased them all, takes but one sense,
And that so lamely, as it leaves behind
A kind of sorrowing dullness to the mind.

     Ah cannot we,
As well as cocks and lions, jocund be
   After such pleasures? Unless wise
Nature decreed – since each such act, they say,
Diminisheth the length of life a day –
   This; as she would man should despise
      The sport,
Because that other curse of being short,

And only for a minute made to be
Eager, desires to raise posterity.

       Since so, my mind
Shall not desire what no man else can find;
   I'll no more dote and run
To pursue things which had endamaged me.
And when I come where moving beauties be,
   As men do when the summer's sun
        Grows great,
Though I admire their greatness, shun their heat.
   Each place can afford shadows. If all fail,
'Tis but applying worm-seed to the tail.

A Fever

O do not die, for I shall hate
   All women so, when thou art gone,
That thee I shall not celebrate,
   When I remember thou wast one.

But yet thou canst not die, I know;
   To leave this world behind, is death;
But when thou from this world wilt go,
   The whole world vapours with thy breath.

Or if, when thou, the world's soul, go'st,
   It stay, 'tis but thy carcase then;
The fairest woman, but thy ghost,
   But corrupt worms, the worthiest men.

O wrangling schools, that search what fire
   Shall burn this world, had none the wit
Unto this knowledge to aspire,
   That this her fever might be it?

And yet she cannot waste by this,
   Nor long bear this torturing wrong,
For much corruption needful is,
   To fuel such a fever long.

These burning fits but meteors be,
   Whose matter in thee is soon spent;
Thy beauty, and all parts, which are thee,
   Are unchangeable firmament.

Yet 'twas of my mind, seizing thee,
  Though it in thee cannot perséver;
For I had rather owner be
  Of thee one hour, than all else ever.

The Flea

Mark but this flea, and mark in this,
How little that which thou deniest me is;
It sucked me first, and now sucks thee,
And in this flea our two bloods mingled be;
Confess it, this cannot be said
A sin, nor shame, or loss of maidenhead,
    Yet this enjoys before it woo,
    And pampered swells with one blood made of two,
    And this, alas, is more than we would do.

Oh stay, three lives in one flea spare,
Where we almost, nay more than married are.
This flea is you and I, and this
Our marriage bed, and marriage temple is;
Though parents grudge, and you, w'are met,
And cloistered in these living walls of jet.
    Though use make you apt to kill me,
    Let not to that, self-murder added be,
    And sacrilege, three sins in killing three.

Cruel and sudden, hast thou since
Purpled thy nail, in blood of innocence?
Wherein could this flea guilty be,
Except in that drop which it sucked from thee?
Yet thou triumph'st, and say'st that thou
Find'st not thyself, nor me the weaker now;
    'Tis true; then learn how false, fears be:
    Just so much honour, when thou yield'st to me,
    Will waste, as this flea's death took life from thee.

The Funeral

Whoever comes to shroud me, do not harm
       Nor question much
That subtle wreath of hair which crowns my arm;
The mystery, the sign, you must not touch;
       For 'tis my outward soul,
Viceroy to that which then to heaven being gone
       Will leave this to control
And keep these limbs, her provinces, from dissolution.

For if the sinewy thread my brain lets fall
       Through every part
Can tie those parts, and make me one of all,
Those hairs which upward grew, and strength and art
       Have from a better brain,
Can better do it; except she meant that I
       By this should know my pain,
As prisoners then are manacled, when they are
    condemn'd to die.

Whate'er she meant by it, bury it with me,
       For since I am
Love's martyr, it might breed idolatry
If into others' hands these relics came.
       As 'twas humility
To afford to it all that a soul can do,
       So 'tis some bravery
That since you would have none of me, I bury some
    of you.

The Good Morrow

I wonder, by my troth, what thou and I
    Did, till we loved? Were we not weaned till then
But sucked on country pleasures, childishly?
    Or snorted we in the seven sleepers' den?
'Twas so; but this, all pleasures fancies be.
If ever any beauty I did see,
Which I desired, and got, 'twas but a dream of thee.

And now good morrow to our waking souls,
    Which watch not one another out of fear;
For love, all love of other sights controls,
    And makes one little room an everywhere.
Let sea-discoverers to new worlds have gone,
Let maps to others, worlds on worlds have shown,
Let us possess one world, each hath one, and is one.

My face in thine eye, thine in mine appears,
    And true plain hearts do in the faces rest;
Where can we find two better hemispheres,
    Without sharp North, without declining West?
Whatever dies was not mixed equally;
If our two loves be one, or, thou and I
Love so alike, that none do slacken, none can die.

The Indifferent

I can love both fair and brown;
Her whom abundance melts, and her whom want
    betrays;
Her who loves loneness best, and her who masks and
    plays;
Her whom the country form'd, and whom the town;
Her who believes, and her who tries;
Her who still weeps with spongy eyes,
And her who is dry cork, and never cries.
I can love her, and her, and you, and you;
I can love any, so she be not true.

Will no other vice content you?
Will it not serve your turn to do as did your mothers?
Or have you all old vices spent, and now would find out
    others?
Or doth a fear that men are true torment you?
O we are not, be not you so;
Let me, and do you, twenty know.
Rob me, but bind me not, and let me go.
Must I, who came to travail thorough you,
Grow your fix'd subject, because you are true?

Venus heard me sigh this song,
And by love's sweetest part, variety, she swore,
She heard not this till now; and that it should be so no
    more.
She went, examined, and return'd ere long,
And said, 'Alas, some two or three
Poor heretics in love there be,

Which think to 'stablish dangerous constancy.
But I have told them, "Since you will be true,
You shall be true to them who are false to you."'

A Jet Ring Sent

Thou art not so black as my heart,
Nor half so brittle as her heart, thou art;
What wouldst thou say? shall both our properties by thee
    be spoke,
  Nothing more endless, nothing sooner broke?

  Marriage rings are not of this stuff;
O why should ought less precious, or less tough
Figure our loves? except in thy name thou have bid it say,
  'I am cheap, and naught but fashion; fling me away.'

Yet stay with me since thou art come,
Circle this finger's top, which did'st her thumb;
Be justly proud, and gladly safe, that thou dost dwell with
    me;
  She that, O, broke her faith, would soon break thee.

A Lecture upon the Shadow

Stand still, and I will read to thee
A lecture, love, in love's philosophy.
   These three hours that we have spent,
   Walking here, two shadows went
Along with us, which we ourselves produc'd.
But, now the sun is just above our head,
   We do those shadows tread,
   And to brave clearness all things are reduc'd.
  So whilst our infant loves did grow,
  Disguises did, and shadows, flow
  From us, and our cares; but now 'tis not so.
That love hath not attain'd the highest degree,
Which is still diligent lest others see.

Except our loves at this noon stay,
We shall new shadows make the other way.
   As the first were made to blind
   Others, these which come behind
Will work upon ourselves, and blind our eyes.
If our loves faint, and westwardly decline;
   To me thou, falsely, thine,
   And I to thee mine actions shall disguise.
  The morning shadows wear away,
  But these grow longer all the day;
  But O, love's day is short, if love decay.
Love is a growing, or full constant light,
And his first minute, after noon, is night.

The Legacy

When I died last, and, dear, I die
  As often as from thee I go,
  Though it be but an hour ago—
And lovers' hours be full eternity—
I can remember yet, that I
  Something did say, and something did bestow;
Though I be dead, which sent me, I should be
Mine own executor and legacy.

I heard me say, 'Tell her anon,
  That myself, that is you, not I,
  Did kill me,' and when I felt me die,
I bid me send my heart when I was gone;
But alas could there find none;
  When I had ripp'd me, and search'd where hearts
    should lie,
It kill'd me again, that I who still was true,
In life, in my last will should cozen you.

Yet I found something like a heart,
  But colours it, and corners had;
  It was not good, it was not bad,
It was entire to none, and few had part.
As good as could be made by art
  It seem'd; and therefore for our losses sad,
I meant to send that heart instead of mine,
But O, no man could hold it, for 'twas thine.

Lovers' Infiniteness

If yet I have not all thy love,
Dear, I shall never have it all;
I cannot breathe one other sigh, to move,
Nor can intreat one other tear to fall.
And all my treasure, which should purchase thee—
Sighs, tears, and oaths, and letters—I have spent.
Yet no more can be due to me,
Than at the bargain made was meant.
If then thy gift of love were partial,
That some to me, some should to others fall,
    Dear, I shall never have thee all.

Or if then thou gavest me all,
All was but all, which thou hadst then;
But if in thy heart, since, there be or shall
New love created be, by other men,
Which have their stocks entire, and can in tears,
In sighs, in oaths, and letters, outbid me,
This new love may beget new fears,
For this love was not vow'd by thee.
And yet it was, thy gift being general;
The ground, thy heart, is mine; whatever shall
    Grow there, dear, I should have it all.

Yet I would not have all yet,
He that hath all can have no more;
And since my love doth every day admit
New growth, thou shouldst have new rewards in store;
Thou canst not every day give me thy heart,
If thou canst give it, then thou never gavest it;

Love's riddles are, that though thy heart depart,
It stays at home, and thou with losing savest it;
But we will have a way more liberal
Than changing hearts, to join them; so we shall
    Be one, and one another's all.

Love's Alchemy

Some that have deeper digg'd love's mine than I,
Say, where his centric happiness doth lie.
    I have loved, and got, and told,
But should I love, get, tell, till I were old,
I should not find that hidden mystery.
    O, 'tis imposture all!
And as no chemic yet th' elixir got,
    But glorifies his pregnant pot
    If by the way to him befall
Some odoriferous thing, or medicinal,
  So, lovers dream a rich and long delight,
  But get a winter-seeming summer's night.

Our ease, our thrift, our honour, and our day,
Shall we for this vain bubble's shadow pay?
    Ends love in this, that my man
    Can be as happy' as I can, if he can
Endure the short scorn of a bridegroom's play?
    That loving wretch that swears
'Tis not the bodies marry, but the minds,
    Which he in her angelic finds,
    Would swear as justly that he hears,
In that day's rude hoarse minstrelsy, the spheres.
  Hope not for mind in women; at their best
  Sweetness and wit, they' are but mummy, possess'd.

Love's Deity

I long to talk with some old lover's ghost,
    Who died before the god of love was born.
I cannot think that he, who then lov'd most,
    Sunk so low as to love one which did scorn.
But since this god produc'd a destiny,
And that vice-nature, custom, lets it be,
    I must love her, that loves not me.

    Sure, they which made him god, meant not
        so much,
    Nor he in his young godhead practised it.
But when an even flame two hearts did touch,
    His office was indulgently to fit
Actives to passives. Correspondency
Only his subject was; it cannot be
    Love, till I love her, that loves me.

    But every modern god will now extend
        His vast prerogative as far as Jove.
To rage, to lust, to write to, to commend,
    All is the purlieu of the god of love.
O, were we waken'd by this tyranny
To ungod this child again, it could not be
    I should love her, who loves not me.

Rebel and atheist too, why murmur I,
As though I felt the worst that love could do?
Love might make me leave loving, or might try
A deeper plague, to make her love me too;
Which, since she loves before, I am loth to see.
Falsehood is worse than hate; and that must be,
If she whom I love, should love me.

Love's Diet

To what a cumbersome unwieldiness
And burdenous corpulence my love had grown,
  But that I did, to make it less,
  And keep it in proportion,
Give it a diet, made it feed upon
That which love worst endures, discretion

Above one sigh a day I allow'd him not,
Of which my fortune, and my faults had part;
  And if sometimes by stealth he got
  A she sigh from my mistress' heart,
And thought to feast upon that, I let him see
'Twas neither very sound, nor meant to me.

If he wrung from me a tear, I brined it so
With scorn and shame, that him it nourish'd not;
  If he suck'd hers, I let him know
  'Twas not a tear which he had got;
His drink was counterfeit, as was his meat;
For eyes, which roll towards all, weep not, but sweat.

Whatever he would dictate I writ that,
But burnt her letters when she writ to me;
  And if that favour made him fat,
  I said, 'If any title be
Convey'd by this, ah! what doth it avail,
To be the fortieth name in an entail?'

Thus I reclaim'd my buzzard love, to fly
At what, and when, and how, and where I choose.
   Now negligent of sports I lie,
    And now, as other falconers use,
I spring a mistress, swear, write, sigh, and weep;
And the game kill'd, or lost, go talk or sleep.

Love's Exchange

Love, any devil else but you
Would for a given soul give something too.
At court your fellows every day
Give th' art of rhyming, huntsmanship, or play,
For them who were their own before;
Only I have nothing, which gave more,
But am, alas ! by being lowly, lower.

I ask no dispensation now,
To falsify a tear, or sigh, or vow;
I do not sue from thee to draw
A *non obstante* on nature's law;
These are prerogatives, they inhere
In thee and thine; none should forswear
Except that he Love's minion were.

Give me thy weakness, make me blind,
Both ways, as thou and thine, in eyes and mind;
Love, let me never know that this
Is love, or, that love childish is;
Let me not know that others know
That she knows my paines, lest that so
A tender shame make me mine own new woe.

If thou give nothing, yet thou'art just,
Because I would not thy first motions trust;
Small towns which stand stiff, till great shot
Enforce them, by war's law condition not;
Such in Love's warfare is my case;

I may not article for grace,
Having put Love at last to show this face.

This face, by which he could command
And change th' idolatry of any land,
This face, which, wheresoe'er it comes,
Can call vow'd men from cloisters, dead from tombs,
And melt both poles at once, and store
Deserts with cities, and make more
Mines in the earth, than quarries were before.

For this Love is enraged with me,
Yet kills not; if I must example be
To future rebels, if th' unborn
Must learn by my being cut up and torn,
Kill, and dissect me, Love; for this
Torture against thine own end is;
Rack'd carcasses make ill anatomies.

Love's Growth

I scarce believe my love to be so pure
    As I had thought it was,
    Because it doth endure
Vicissitude, and season, as the grass;
Methinks I lied all winter, when I swore
My love was infinite, if spring make' it more.

But if this medicine, love, which cures all sorrow
    With more, not only be no quintessence,
    But mix'd of all stuffs vexing soul or sense,
And of the sun his active vigour borrow,
Love's not so pure and abstract as they use
To say, which have no mistress but their Muse;
But as all else, being elemented too,
Love sometimes would contemplate, sometimes do.

And yet no greater, but more eminent,
    Love by the spring is grown;
    As, in the firmament,
Stars by the sun are not enlarged, but shown,
Gentle love deeds, as blossoms on a bough,
From love's awakened root do bud out now.

If, as in water stirr'd more circles be
    Produced by one, love such additions take,
    Those, like so many spheres, but one heaven make,
For they are all concentric unto thee;
And though each spring do add to love new heat,

As princes do in times of action get
New taxes, and remit them not in peace,
No winter shall abate this spring's increase.

Love's Usury

For every hour that thou wilt spare me now,
    I will allow,
Usurious god of love, twenty to thee,
When with my brown my grey hairs equal be.
Till then, Love, let my body range, and let
Me travel, sojourn, snatch, plot, have, forget,
Resume my last year's relict; think that yet
    We'd never met.

Let me think any rival's letter mine,
    And at next nine
Keep midnight's promise; mistake by the way
The maid, and tell the lady of that delay;
Only let me love none; no, not the sport
From country grass to confitures of court,
Or city's *quelque-choses*; let not report
    My mind transport.

This bargain's good; if when I'm old, I be
    Inflamed by thee,
If thine own honour, or my shame and pain,
Thou covet most, at that age thou shalt gain.
Do thy will then; then subject and degree
And fruit of love, Love, I submit to thee.
Spare me till then; I'll bear it, though she be
    One that love me.

The Message

Send home my long stray'd eyes to me,
Which, O, too long have dwelt on thee;
Yet since there they have learn'd such ill,
    Such forced fashions,
    And false passions,
        That they be
        Made by thee
Fit for no good sight, keep them still.

Send home my harmless heart again,
Which no unworthy thought could stain;
Which if it be taught by thine
    To make jestings
    Of protestings,
        And break both
        Word and oath,
Keep it, for then 'tis none of mine.

Yet send me back my heart and eyes,
That I may know, and see thy lies,
And may laugh and joy, when thou
    Art in anguish
    And dost languish
        For some one
        That will none,
Or prove as false as thou art now.

Negative Love

I never stoop'd so low, as they
Which on an eye, cheek, lip, can prey;
   Seldom to them which soar no higher
   Than virtue, or the mind to admire.
For sense and understanding may
   Know what gives fuel to their fire;
My love, though silly, is more brave;
For may I miss, whene'er I crave,
If I know yet what I would have.

If that be simply perfectest,
Which can by no way be express'd
   But negatives, my love is so.
   To all, which all love, I say no.
If any who deciphers best,
   What we know not—ourselves—can know,
Let him teach me that nothing. This
As yet my ease and comfort is,
Though I speed not, I cannot miss.

A Nocturnal upon St Lucy's Day,
Being the Shortest Day

'Tis the year's midnight, and it is the day's,
Lucy's, who scarce seven hours herself unmasks;
   The sun is spent, and now his flasks
   Send forth light squibs, no constant rays;
     The world's whole sap is sunk;
The general balm th' hydroptic earth hath drunk,
Whither, as to the bed's-feet, life is shrunk,
Dead and interr'd; yet all these seem to laugh,
Compared with me, who am their epitaph.

Study me then, you who shall lovers be
At the next world, that is, at the next spring;
   For I am every dead thing,
   In whom Love wrought new alchemy.
     For his art did express
A quintessence even from nothingness,
From dull privations, and lean emptiness;
He ruin'd me, and I am re-begot
Of absence, darkness, death: things which are not.

All others, from all things, draw all that's good,
Life, soul, form, spirit, whence they being have;
   I, by Love's limbec, am the grave
   Of all that's nothing. Oft a flood
     Have we two wept, and so
Drown'd the whole world, us two; oft did we grow
To be two chaoses, when we did show
Care to aught else; and often absences
Withdrew our souls, and made us carcasses.

But I am by her death (which word wrongs her)
Of the first nothing the elixir grown;
  Were I a man, that I were one
  I needs must know; I should prefer,
    If I were any beast,
Some ends, some means; yea plants, yea stones detest,
And love; all, all some properties invest;
If I an ordinary nothing were,
As shadow, a light, and body must be here.

But I am none; nor will my sun renew.
You lovers, for whose sake the lesser sun
  At this time to the Goat is run
  To fetch new lust, and give it you,
    Enjoy your summer all
Since she enjoys her long night's festival;
Let me prepare towards her, and let me call
This hour her vigil, and her eve, since this
Both the year's, and the day's deep midnight is.

The Paradox

No lover saith, I love, nor any other
   Can judge a perfect lover;
He thinks that else none can or will agree,
   That any loves but he;
I cannot say I loved, for who can say
   He was kill'd yesterday?
Love with excess of heat, more young than old,
   Death kills with too much cold;
We die but once, and who loved last did die,
   He that saith, twice, doth lie;
For though he seem to move, and stir a while,
   It doth the sense beguile.
Such life is like the light which bideth yet
   When the life's light is set,
Or like the heat which fire in solid matter
   Leaves behind, two hours after.
Once I loved and died; and am now become
   Mine epitaph and tomb;
Here dead men speak their last, and so do I;
   Love-slain, lo, here I lie.

The Primrose, Being at Montgomery Castle, upon the Hill, on which it is Situate

Upon this primrose hill,
 Where, if heaven would distil
A shower of rain, each several drop might go
To his own primrose, and grow manna so;
And where their form, and their infinity
 Make a terrestrial galaxy,
 As the small stars do in the sky;
I walk to find a true love; and I see
That 'tis not a mere woman, that is she,
But must or more or less than woman be.

Yet know I not, which flower
 I wish; a six, or four;
For should my true-love less than woman be,
She were scarce anything; and then, should she
Be more than woman, she would get above
 All thought of sex, and think to move
 My heart to study her, and not to love.
Both these were monsters; since there must reside
Falsehood in woman, I could more abide,
She were by art, than nature falsified.

Live, primrose, then, and thrive
 With thy true number, five;
And, woman, whom this flower doth represent,
With this mysterious number be content;
Ten is the farthest number; if half ten
 Belong unto each woman, then
 Each woman may take half us men;

Or—if this will not serve their turn—since all
Numbers are odd or even, and they fall
First into five, women may take us all.

The Prohibition

Take heed of loving me;
At least remember, I forbade it thee;
  Not that I shall repair my unthrifty waste
Of breath and blood, upon thy sighs and tears,
  By being to thee then what to me thou wast;
But so great joy our life at once outwears.
  Then, lest thy love by my death frustrate be,
  If thou love me, take heed of loving me.

Take heed of hating me,
Or too much triumph in the victory;
  Not that I shall be mine own officer,
And hate with hate again retaliate;
  But thou wilt lose the style of conqueror,
If I, thy conquest, perish by thy hate.
  Then, lest my being nothing lessen thee,
  If thou hate me, take heed of hating me.

Yet love and hate me too;
So these extremes shall ne'er their office do;
  Love me, that I may die the gentler way;
Hate me, because thy love's too great for me;
  Or let these two, themselves, not me, decay;
So shall I live thy stage, not triumph be.
  Lest thou thy love and hate and me undo,
  To let me live, O love and hate me too.

The Relic

When my grave is broke up again
Some second guest to entertain,
(For graves have learn'd that woman-head,
To be to more than one a bed)
    And he that digs it, spies
A bracelet of bright hair about the bone,
    Will he not let' us alone,
And think that there a loving couple lies,
Who thought that this device might be some way
To make their souls, at the last busy day
Meet at this grave, and make a little stay?

If this fall in a time, or land,
Where mis-devotion doth command,
Then he, that digs us up, will bring
Us to the bishop and the king,
    To make us relics; then
Thou shalt be a Mary Magdalen, and I
    A something else thereby;
All women shall adore us, and some men;
And since at such time miracles are sought,
I would have that age by this paper taught
What miracles we harmless lovers wrought.

First, we loved well and faithfully,
Yet knew not what we loved, nor why;
Difference of sex no more we knew,
Than our guardian angels do;
    Coming and going, we
Perchance might kiss, but not between those meals;

Our hands ne'er touch'd the seals,
Which nature, injured by late law, sets free.
These miracles we did; but now, alas!
All measure, and all language, I should pass,
Should I tell what a miracle she was.

Self Love

He that cannot choose but love,
　And strives against it still,
Never shall my fancy move,
　For he loves against his will;

Nor he which is all his own,
　And cannot pleasure choose;
When I am caught he can be gone,
　And when he list refuse;

Nor he that loves none but fair,
　For such by all are sought;
Nor he that can for foul ones care,
　For his judgement then is nought;

Nor he that hath wit, for he
　Will make me his jest or slave;
Nor a fool when others —
　He can neither —

Nor he that still his mistress pays,
　For she is thrall'd therefore;
Nor he that pays not, for he says
　Within, she's worth no more.

Is there then no kind of men
　Whom I may freely prove?
I will vent that humour then
　In mine own self love.

Song

Go and catch a falling star,
   Get with child a mandrake root,
Tell me where all past years are,
   Or who cleft the devil's foot,
Teach me to hear mermaids singing,
Or to keep off envy's stinging,
         And find
         What wind
Serves to advance an honest mind.

If thou be'est born to strange sights,
   Things invisible to see,
Ride ten thousand days and nights,
   Till age snow white hairs on thee,
Thou, when thou return'st, wilt tell me
All strange wonders that befell thee,
         And swear,
         No where
Lives a woman true, and fair.

If thou find'st one, let me know,
   Such a pilgrimage were sweet;
Yet do not, I would not go,
   Though at next door we might meet;
Though she were true when you met her,
And last, till you write your letter,
         Yet she
         Will be
False, ere I come, to two, or three.

Song

Sweetest love, I do not go,
  For weariness of thee,
Nor in hope the world can show
  A fitter love for me;
   But since that I
Must die at last, 'tis best,
To use myself in jest
  Thus by feigned deaths to die.

Yesternight the sun went hence,
  And yet is here today;
He hath no desire nor sense,
  Nor half so short a way;
   Then fear not me,
But believe that I shall make
Speedier journeys, since I take
  More wings and spurs than he.

O how feeble is man's power,
  That if good fortune fall,
Cannot add another hour,
  Nor a lost hour recall!
   But come bad chance,
And we join to' it our strength,
And we teach it art and length,
  Itself o'er us to' advance.

When thou sigh'st, thou sigh'st not wind,
  But sigh'st my soul away;
When thou weep'st, unkindly kind,

My life's blood doth decay.
   It cannot be
That thou lovest me, as thou say'st,
If in thine my life thou waste,
   Thou art the best of me.

Let not thy divining heart
   Forethink me any ill;
Destiny may take thy part,
   And may thy fears fulfil;
     But think that we
Are but turned aside to sleep;
They who one another keep
   Alive, ne'er parted be.

The Sun Rising

Busy old fool, unruly sun,
Why dost thou thus,
Through windows, and through curtains call on us?
Must to thy motions lovers' seasons run?
Saucy pedantic wretch, go chide
Late school boys and sour prentices,
Go tell court huntsmen that the king will ride,
Call country ants to harvest offices,
Love, all alike, no season knows nor clime,
Nor hours, days, months, which are the rags of time.

Thy beams, so reverend and strong
Why shouldst thou think?
I could eclipse and cloud them with a wink,
But that I would not lose her sight so long;
If her eyes have not blinded thine,
Look, and tomorrow late, tell me,
Whether both th' Indias of spice and mine
Be where thou leftst them, or lie here with me.
Ask for those kings whom thou saw'st yesterday,
And thou shalt hear, All here in one bed lay.

She's all states, and all princes, I,
Nothing else is.
Princes do but play us; compared to this,
All honour's mimic, all wealth alchemy.
Thou, sun, art half as happy as we,
In that the world's contracted thus.

Thine age asks ease, and since thy duties be
To warm the world, that's done in warming us.
Shine here to us, and thou art everywhere;
This bed thy centre is, these walls, thy sphere.

The Token

Send me some tokens, that my hope may live
  Or that my easeless thoughts may sleep and rest;
Send me some honey, to make sweet my hive,
  That in my passions I may hope the best.
I beg no ribbon wrought with thine own hands,
  To knit our loves in the fantastic strain
Of new-touch'd youth; nor ring to show the stands
  Of our affection, that as that's round and plain,
So should our loves meet in simplicity;
  No, nor the corals, which thy wrist enfold,
Laced up together in congruity,
  To show our thoughts should rest in the same hold;
No, nor thy picture, though most gracious,
  And most desired, 'cause 'tis like the best;
Nor witty lines, which are most copious,
  Within the writings which thou hast address'd.
Send me nor this nor that to increase my score,
But swear thou think'st I love thee, and no more.

The Triple Fool

I am two fools, I know,
  For loving, and for saying so
    In whining poetry;
But where's that wiseman, that would not be I,
    If she would not deny?
Then as th' earth's inward narrow crooked lanes
  Do purge sea water's fretful salt away,
I thought, if I could draw my pains
  Through rhyme's vexation, I should them allay.
Grief brought to numbers cannot be so fierce,
For he tames it, that fetters it in verse.

But when I have done so,
  Some man, his art and voice to show,
    Doth set and sing my pain;
And, by delighting many, frees again
  Grief, which verse did restrain.
To love and grief tribute of verse belongs,
  But not of such as pleases when 'tis read.
Both are increasèd by such songs,
  For both their triumphs so are published,
And I, which was two fools, do so grow three.
Who are a little wise, the best fools be.

Twicknam Garden

Blasted with sighs, and surrounded with tears,
   Hither I come to seek the spring,
   And at mine eyes, and at mine ears,
Receive such balms as else cure everything;
   But O, self-traitor, I do bring
The spider love, which transubstantiates all,
   And can convert manna to gall;
And that this place may thoroughly be thought
True paradise, I have the serpent brought.

'Twere wholesomer for me that winter did
   Benight the glory of this place,
   And that a grave frost did forbid
These trees to laugh, and mock me to my face;
   But that I may not this disgrace
Endure, nor yet leave loving, Love, let me
   Some senseless piece of this place be;
Make me a mandrake, so I may grow here,
Or a stone fountain weeping out my year.

Hither with crystal phials lovers come,
   And take my tears, which are love's wine,
   And try your mistress' tears at home,
For all are false, that taste not just like mine.
   Alas ! hearts do not in eyes shine,
Nor can you more judge woman's thoughts by tears,
   Than by her shadow what she wears.
O perverse sex, where none is true but she,
Who's therefore true, because her truth kills me.

The Undertaking

I have done one braver thing
  Than all the Worthies did;
And yet a braver thence doth spring,
  Which is, to keep that hid.

It were but madness now to impart
  The skill of specular stone,
When he, which can have learn'd the art
  To cut it, can find none.

So, if I now should utter this,
  Others—because no more
Such stuff to work upon, there is—
  Would love but as before.

But he who loveliness within
  Hath found, all outward loathes,
For he who colour loves, and skin,
  Loves but their oldest clothes.

If, as I have, you also do
  Virtue in woman see,
And dare love that, and say so too,
  And forget the He and She;

And if this love, though placèd so,
  From profane men you hide,
Which will no faith on this bestow,
  Or, if they do, deride:

Then you have done a braver thing
  Than all the Worthies did;
And a braver thence will spring,
  Which is, to keep that hid.

A Valediction: Forbidding Mourning

As virtuous men pass mildly away,
   And whisper to their souls to go,
Whilst some of their sad friends do say
   The breath goes now, and some say, No:

So let us melt, and make no noise,
   No tear-floods, nor sigh-tempests move;
'Twere profanation of our joys
   To tell the laity our love.

Moving of th' earth brings harms and fears,
   Men reckon what it did, and meant;
But trepidation of the spheres,
   Though greater far, is innocent.

Dull sublunary lovers' love
   (Whose soul is sense) cannot admit
Absence, because it doth remove
   Those things which elemented it.

But we by a love so much refined,
   That our selves know not what it is,
Inter-assured of the mind,
   Care less, eyes, lips, and hands to miss.

Our two souls therefore, which are one,
   Though I must go, endure not yet
A breach, but an expansion,
   Like gold to airy thinness beat.

If they be two, they are two so
   As stiff twin compasses are two;
Thy soul, the fixed foot, makes no show
   To move, but doth, if the other do.

And though it in the centre sit,
   Yet when the other far doth roam,
It leans and hearkens after it,
   And grows erect, as that comes home.

Such wilt thou be to me, who must,
   Like th' other foot, obliquely run;
Thy firmness makes my circle just,
   And makes me end where I begun.

A Valediction: of the Book

I'll tell thee now (dear Love) what thou shalt do
    To anger destiny, as she doth us;
    How I shall stay, though she esloign me thus,
And how posterity shall know it too;
    How thine may out-endure
    Sibyl's glory, and obscure
    Her who from Pindar could allure,
  And her, through whose help Lucan is not lame,
And her, whose book (they say) Homer did find, and
        name.

Study our manuscripts, those myriads
    Of letters, which have past twixt thee and me;
    Thence write our annals, and in them will be
To all whom love's subliming fire invades,
    Rule and example found;
    There, the faith of any ground
    No schismatic will dare to wound,
  That sees, how Love this grace to us affords,
To make, to keep, to use, to be these his records.

This book, as long-lived as the elements,
    Or as the world's form, this all-gravèd tome
    In cypher writ, or new made idiom;
We for love's clergy only' are instruments;
    When this book is made thus,
    Should again the ravenous
    Vandals and Goths invade us,
  Learning were safe; in this our universe,
Schools might learn sciences, spheres music, angels verse.

Here Love's divines (since all divinity
    Is love or wonder) may find all they seek,
    Whether abstract spiritual love they like,
Their souls exhaled with what they do not see;
    Or, loth so to amuse
    Faith's infirmity, they choose
    Something which they may see and use;
  For, though mind be the heaven, where love doth sit,
Beauty' a convenient type may be to figure it.

Here more than in their books may lawyers find,
    Both by what titles mistresses are ours,
    And how prerogative these states devours,
Transferr'd from Love himself, to womankind;
    Who though from heart, and eyes,
    They exact great subsidies,
    Forsake him who on them relies,
  And for the cause, honour, or conscience give,
Chimeras, vain as they, or their prerogative.

Here statesmen (or of them, they which can read)
    May of their occupation find the grounds,
    Love and their art alike it deadly wounds,
If to consider what 'tis, one proceed.
    In both they do excel
    Who the present govern well,
    Whose weakness none doth, or dares tell;
  In this thy book, such will there nothing see,
As in the Bible some can find out alchemy.

Thus vent thy thoughts; abroad I'll study thee,
    As he removes far off, that great heights takes;

How great love is, presence best trial makes,
But absence tries how long this love will be;
   To take a latitude
   Sun, or stars, are fitliest viewed
   At their brightest, but to conclude,
  Of longitudes, what other way have we,
But to mark when and where the dark eclipses be?

A Valediction: of My Name in the Window

I

My name engraved herein
Doth contribute my firmness to this glass,
Which ever since that charm hath been
As hard, as that which graved it was;
Thine eye will give it price enough, to mock
The diamonds of either rock.

II

'Tis much that glass should be
As all-confessing, and through-shine as I;
'Tis more that it shows thee to thee,
And clear reflects thee to thine eye.
But all such rules love's magic can undo;
Here you see me, and I am you.

III

As no one point, nor dash,
Which are but accessories to this name,
The showers and tempests can outwash,
So shall all times find me the same;
You this entireness better may fulfill,
Who have the pattern with you still.

IV

Or if too hard and deep
This learning be, for a scratch'd name to teach,
It as a given death's head keep,
Lovers' mortality to preach;
Or think this ragged bony name to be
My ruinous anatomy.

V

Then, as all my souls be
Emparadised in you—in whom alone
I understand, and grow, and see—
The rafters of my body, bone,
Being still with you, the muscle, sinew, and vein
Which tile this house, will come again.

VI

Till my return repair
And recompact my scatter'd body so,
As all the virtuous powers which are
Fix'd in the stars are said to flow
Into such characters as gravèd be
When these stars have supremacy.

VII

So since this name was cut,
When love and grief their exaltation had,
No door 'gainst this name's influence shut.
As much more loving, as more sad,
'Twill make thee; and thou shouldst, till I return,
Since I die daily, daily mourn.

VIII

When thy inconsiderate hand
Flings open this casement, with my trembling name,
To look on one, whose wit or land
New battery to thy heart may frame,
Then think this name alive, and that thou thus
In it offend'st my Genius.

IX

And when thy melted maid,
Corrupted by thy lover's gold and page,
His letter at thy pillow hath laid,
Disputed it, and tamed thy rage,
And thou begin'st to thaw towards him, for this,
May my name step in, and hide his.

X

And if this treason go
To an overt act and that thou write again,
In superscribing, this name flow
Into thy fancy from the pane;
So, in forgetting thou rememb'rest right,
And unaware to me shalt write.

XI

But glass and lines must be
No means our firm substantial love to keep;
Near death inflicts this lethargy,
And this I murmur in my sleep;
Impute this idle talk, to that I go,
For dying men talk often so.

A Valediction: of Weeping

> Let me pour forth
> My tears before thy face, whilst I stay here,
> For thy face coins them, and thy stamp they bear,
> And by this mintage they are something worth,
>> For thus they be
>> Pregnant of thee;
> Fruits of much grief they are, emblems of more;
> When a tear falls, that thou falls which it bore;
> So thou and I are nothing then, when on a divers shore.

> On a round ball
> A workman that hath copies by, can lay
> An Europe, Afric, and an Asia,
> And quickly make that, which was nothing, all;
>> So doth each tear,
>> Which thee doth wear,
> A globe, yea world, by that impression grow,
> Till thy tears mix'd with mine do overflow
> This world; by waters sent from thee, my heaven
>> dissolvèd so.

> O more than moon,
> Draw not up seas to drown me in thy sphere;
> Weep me not dead, in thine arms, but forbear
> To teach the sea what it may do too soon;
>> Let not the wind
>> Example find
> To do me more harm than it purposeth:
> Since thou and I sigh one another's breath,
> Whoe'er sighs most is cruellest, and hastes the other's
>> death.

The Will

Before I sigh my last gasp, let me breathe,
Great Love, some legacies; I here bequeath
Mine eyes to Argus, if mine eyes can see;
If they be blind, then, Love, I give them thee;
My tongue to Fame; to ambassadors mine ears;
To women, or the sea, my tears;
Thou, Love, hast taught me heretofore
By making me serve her who had twenty more,
That I should give to none, but such as had
too much before.

My constancy I to the planets give;
My truth to them who at the court do live;
My ingenuity and openness,
To Jesuits; to buffoons my pensiveness;
My silence to any, who abroad hath been;
My money to a Capuchin:
Thou, Love, taught'st me, by appointing me
To love there, where no love received can be,
Only to give to such as have an incapacity.

My faith I give to Roman Catholics;
All my good works unto the Schismatics
Of Amsterdam; my best civility
And courtship to an University;
My modesty I give to soldiers bare;
My patience let gamesters share:
Thou, Love, taught'st me, by making me
Love her that holds my love disparity,
Only to give to those that count my gifts indignity.

I give my reputation to those
Which were my friends; mine industry to foes;
To schoolmen I bequeath my doubtfulness;
My sickness to physicians, or excess;
To nature all that I in rhyme have writ;
And to my company my wit:
Thou, Love, by making me adore
Her, who begot this love in me before,
Taught'st me to make, as though I gave, when I
do but restore.

To him for whom the passing-bell next tolls,
I give my physic books; my written rolls
Of moral counsels I to Bedlam give;
My brazen medals unto them which live
In want of bread; to them which pass among
All foreigners, mine English tongue:
Though, Love, by making me love one
Who thinks her friendship a fit portion
For younger lovers, dost my gifts thus disproportion.

Therefore I'll give no more, but I'll undo
The world by dying, because love dies too.
Then all your beauties will be no more worth
Than gold in mines, where none doth draw it forth;
And all your graces no more use shall have,
Than a sun-dial in a grave:
Thou, Love, taught'st me by making me
Love her who doth neglect both me and thee,
To invent, and practise this one way, to annihilate
all three.

Witchcraft by a Picture

I fix mine eye on thine, and there
  Pity my picture burning in thine eye;
My picture drown'd in a transparent tear,
  When I look lower I espy;
    Hadst thou the wicked skill
By pictures made and marr'd, to kill,
How many ways mightst thou perform thy will?

But now I've drunk thy sweet salt tears,
  And though thou pour more, I'll depart;
My picture vanished, vanish all fears
  That I can be endamaged by that art;
    Though thou retain of me
One picture more, yet that will be,
Being in thine own heart, from all malice free.

Woman's Constancy

Now thou hast loved me one whole day,
Tomorrow when thou leav'st, what wilt thou say?
Wilt thou then antedate some new-made vow?
      Or say that now
We are not just those persons which we were?
Or, that oaths made in reverential fear
Of Love, and his wrath, any may forswear?
Or, as true deaths true marriages untie,
So lovers' contracts, images of those,
Bind but till sleep, death's image, them unloose?
      Or, your own end to justify,
For having purposed change and falsehood, you
Can have no way but falsehood to be true?
Vain lunatic, against these 'scapes I could
      Dispute, and conquer, if I would,
      Which I abstain to do,
For by tomorrow, I may think so too.

SECTION II:
ELEGIES

ELEGY I

Jealousy

Fond woman, which wouldst have thy husband die,
And yet complain'st of his great jealousy;
If, swollen with poison, he lay in his last bed,
His body with a sere bark covered,
Drawing his breath as quick and short as can
The nimblest crocheting musician,
Ready with loathsome vomiting to spew
His soul out of one hell into a new,
Made deaf with his poor kindred's howling cries,
Begging with few feigned tears great legacies—
Thou wouldst not weep, but jolly, and frolic be,
As a slave, which tomorrow should be free.
Yet weep'st thou, when thou seest him hungerly
Swallow his own death, heart's-bane jealousy?
O give him many thanks, he's courteous,
That in suspecting kindly warneth us.
We must not, as we used, flout openly,
In scoffing riddles, his deformity;
Nor at his board together being sat,
With words, nor touch, scarce looks, adulterate.
Nor when he, swollen and pamper'd with great fare,
Sits down and snorts, caged in his basket chair,
Must we usurp his own bed any more,
Nor kiss and play in his house, as before.
Now I see many dangers; for it is
His realm, his castle, and his diocese.
But if—as envious men, which would revile
Their prince, or coin his gold, themselves exile

Into another country, and do it there—
We play in another house, what should we fear?
Then we will scorn his household policies,
His silly plots, and pensionary spies,
As the inhabitants of Thames' right side
Do London's mayor, or Germans the Pope's pride.

ELEGY II

The Anagram

Marry, and love thy Flavia, for she
Hath all things, whereby others beauteous be;
For, though her eyes be small, her mouth is great;
Though they be ivory, yet her teeth be jet;
Though they be dim, yet she is light enough;
And though her harsh hair fall, her skin is tough;
What though her cheeks be yellow, her hair's red,
Give her thine, and she hath a maidenhead.
These things are beauty's elements, where these
Meet in one, that one must, as perfect, please.
If red and white, and each good quality
Be in thy wench, ne'er ask where it doth lie.
In buying things perfumed, we ask, if there
Be musk and amber in it, but not where.
Though all her parts be not in th' usual place,
She hath yet an anagram of a good face.
If we might put the letters but one way,
In that lean dearth of words, what could we say?
When by the gamut some musicians make
A perfect song, others will undertake,
By the same gamut changed, to equal it.
Things simply good can never be unfit;
She's fair as any, if all be like her;
And if none be, then she is singular.
All love is wonder; if we justly do
Account her wonderful, why not lovely too?
Love built on beauty, soon as beauty, dies;
Choose this face, changed by no deformities.

Women are like angels; the fair be
Like those which fell to worse; but such as she,
Like to good angels, nothing can impair:
'Tis less grief to be foul, than to have been fair.
For one night's revels, silk and gold we choose,
But, in long journeys, cloth and leather use.
Beauty is barren oft; best husbands say
There is best land, where there is foulest way.
O, what a sovereign plaster will she be,
If thy past sins have taught thee jealousy!
Here needs no spies, nor eunuchs; her commit
Safe to thy foes, yea, to a marmoset.
Like Belgia's cities the round country drowns,
That dirty foulness guards and arms the towns,
So doth her face guard her; and so, for thee,
Which forced by business absent oft must be,
She, whose face, like clouds, turns the day to night;
Who, mightier than the sea, makes Moors seem white;
Who, though seven years she in the stews had laid,
A nunnery durst receive, and think a maid;
And though in childbed's labour she did lie,
Midwives would swear, 'twere but a tympany;
Whom, if she accuse herself, I credit less
Than witches, which impossibles confess;
One like none, and liked of none, fittest were;
For things in fashion every man will wear.

ELEGY III

Change

Although thy hand and faith, and good works too,
Have sealed thy love which nothing should undo,
Yea, though thou fall back, that apostasy
Confirm thy love, yet much, much I fear thee.
Women are like the arts, forced unto none,
Open to all searchers, unprized, if unknown.
If I have caught a bird, and let him fly,
Another fowler using these means, as I,
May catch the same bird; and, as these things be,
Women are made for men, not him nor me.
Foxes and goats—all beasts—change when they please.
Shall women, more hot, wily, wild, than these,
Be bound to one man and did nature then
Idly make them apter to endure than men?
They're our clogs, not their own; if a man be
Chain'd to a galley, yet the galley's free.
Who hath a plough-land, casts all his seed corn there,
And yet allows his ground more corn should bear;
Though Danuby into the sea must flow,
The sea receives the Rhine, Volga, and Po.
By nature, which gave it, this liberty,
Thou lovest, but O! canst thou love it and me?
Likeness glues love; and if that thou so do,
To make us like and love, must I change too?
More than thy hate, I hate it; rather let me
Allow her change, then change as oft as she,
And so not teach, but force my opinion,
To love not any one, nor every one.

To live in one land is captivity,
To run all countries a wild roguery.
Waters stink soon, if in one place they bide,
And in the vast sea are more putrefied;
But when they kiss one bank, and leaving this
Never look back, but the next bank do kiss,
Then are they purest; change is the nursery
Of music, joy, life, and eternity.

ELEGY IV

The Perfume

Once, and but once, found in thy company,
All thy supposed escapes are laid on me;
And as a thief at bar is question'd there
By all the men that have been robb'd that year,
So am I—by this traitorous means surprised—
By thy hydroptic father catechized.
Though he had wont to search with glazed eyes,
As though he came to kill a cockatrice;
Though he hath oft sworn that he would remove
Thy beauty's beauty, and food of our love,
Hope of his goods, if I with thee were seen,
Yet close and secret, as our souls, we've been.
Though thy immortal mother, which doth lie
Still buried in her bed, yet will not die,
Takes this advantage to sleep out daylight,
And watch thy entries and returns all night;
And, when she takes thy hand, and would seem kind,
Doth search what rings and armlets she can find;
And kissing notes the colour of thy face;
And fearing lest thou'rt swollen, doth thee embrace;
To try if thou long, doth name strange meats;
And notes thy paleness, blushing, sighs, and sweats;
And politicly will to thee confess
The sins of her own youth's rank lustiness;
Yet love these sorceries did remove, and move
Thee to gull thine own mother for my love.
Thy little brethren, which like fairy sprites
Oft skipp'd into our chamber, those sweet nights,

And kiss'd, and ingled on thy father's knee,
Were bribed next day to tell what they did see;
The grim-eight-foot-high-iron-bound serving-man,
That oft names God in oaths, and only then,
He that, to bar the first gate, doth as wide
As the great Rhodian Colossus stride
—Which, if in hell no other pains there were,
Makes me fear hell, because he must be there—
Though by thy father he were hired to this,
Could never witness any touch or kiss.
But O! too common ill, I brought with me
That, which betray'd me to mine enemy,
A loud perfume, which at my entrance cried
Even at thy father's nose; so were we spied.
When, like a tyrant king, that in his bed
Smelt gunpowder, the pale wretch shivered,
Had it been some bad smell, he would have thought
That his own feet, or breath, that smell had wrought;
But as we in our isle imprisoned,
Where cattle only and divers dogs are bred,
The precious unicorns strange monsters call,
So thought he good strange, that had none at all.
I taught my silks their whistling to forbear;
Even my oppress'd shoes dumb and speechless were;
Only thou bitter sweet, whom I had laid
Next me, me traitorously hast betray'd,
And unsuspected hast invisibly
At once fled unto him, and stay'd with me.
Base excrement of earth, which dost confound
Sense from distinguishing the sick from sound!
By thee the silly amorous sucks his death
By drawing in a leprous harlot's breath;

By thee, the greatest stain to man's estate
Falls on us, to be call'd effeminate;
Though you be much loved in the prince's hall,
There things that seem exceed substantial;
Gods, when ye fumed on altars, were pleased well,
Because you were burnt, not that they liked your smell;
You're loathsome all, being taken simply alone;
Shall we love ill things join'd, and hate each one?
If you were good, your good doth soon decay;
And you are rare; that takes the good away:
All my perfumes I give most willingly
To embalm thy father's corpse; what? will he die?

ELEGY V

His Picture

Here take my picture; though I bid farewell,
Thine, in my heart, where my soul dwells, shall dwell.
'Tis like me now, but I dead, 'twill be more,
When we are shadows both, than 'twas before.
When weather-beaten I come back; my hand
Perhaps with rude oars torn, or sun-beams tann'd,
My face and breast of haircloth, and my head
With care's harsh sudden hoariness o'erspread,
My body a sack of bones, broken within,
And powder's blue stains scatter'd on my skin;
If rival fools tax thee to have loved a man,
So foul and coarse, as, O, I may seem then,
This shall say what I was; and thou shalt say,
'Do his hurts reach me? doth my worth decay?
Or do they reach his judging mind, that he
Should now love less, what he did love to see?
That which in him was fair and delicate,
Was but the milk, which in love's childish state
Did nurse it; who is now grown strong enough
To feed on that, which to weak tastes seems tough.'

ELEGY VI

O, let me not serve so, as those men serve,
Whom honour's smokes at once fatten and starve,
Poorly enrich'd with great men's words or looks;
Nor so write my name in thy loving books
As those idolatrous flatterers, which still
Their princes' style with many realms fulfil,
Whence they no tribute have, and where no sway.
Such services I offer as shall pay
Themselves; I hate dead names. O, then let me
Favourite in ordinary, or no favourite be.
When my soul was in her own body sheathed,
Nor yet by oaths betroth'd, nor kisses breathed
Into my purgatory, faithless thee,
Thy heart seemed wax, and steel thy constancy.
So careless flowers strew'd on the water's face
The curled whirlpools suck, smack, and embrace,
Yet drown them; so the taper's beamy eye
Amorously twinkling beckons the giddy fly,
Yet burns his wings; and such the devil is,
Scarce visiting them who are entirely his.
When I behold a stream, which from the spring
Doth with doubtful melodious murmuring,
Or in a speechless slumber, calmly ride
Her wedded channel's bosom, and there chide,
And bend her brows, and swell, if any bough
Do but stoop down to kiss her utmost brow;
Yet, if her often gnawing kisses win
The traitorous banks to gape, and let her in,
She rusheth violently, and doth divorce
Her from her native and her long-kept course,

And roars, and braves it, and in gallant scorn,
In flattering eddies promising return,
She flouts her channel, which thenceforth is dry;
Then say I: 'That is she, and this am I.'
Yet let not thy deep bitterness beget
Careless despair in me, for that will whet
My mind to scorn; and O, love dull'd with pain
Was ne'er so wise, nor well arm'd, as disdain.
Then with new eyes I shall survey thee, and spy
Death in thy cheeks, and darkness in thine eye,
Though hope bred faith and love; thus taught, I shall,
As nations do from Rome, from thy love fall;
My hate shall outgrow thine, and utterly
I will renounce thy dalliance; and when I
Am the recusant, in that resolute state
What hurts it me to be excommunicate?

ELEGY VII

Nature's lay idiot, I taught thee to love,
And in that sophistry, O! thou dost prove
Too subtle; fool, thou didst not understand
The mystic language of the eye nor hand;
Nor couldst thou judge the difference of the air
Of sighs, and say, 'This lies, this sounds despair';
Nor by th' eye's water cast a malady
Desperately hot, or changing feverously.
I had not taught thee then the alphabet
Of flowers, how they, devisefully being set
And bound up, might with speechless secrecy
Deliver errands mutely, and mutually.
Remember since all thy words used to be
To every suitor, 'Ay, if my friends agree';
Since household charms, thy husband's name to teach,
Were all the love-tricks that thy wit could reach;
And since an hour's discourse could scarce have made
One answer in thee, and that ill arrayed
In broken proverbs, and torn sentences.
Thou art not by so many duties his—
That from th' world's common having sever'd thee,
Inlaid thee, neither to be seen, nor see—
As mine, who have with amorous delicacies
Refined thee into a blissful paradise.
Thy graces and good works my creatures be;
I planted knowledge and life's tree in thee;
Which O! shall strangers taste? Must I, alas!
Frame and enamel plate, and drink in glass?
Chafe wax for other's seals? break a colt's force,
And leave him then, being made a ready horse?

ELEGY VIII

The Comparison

As the sweet sweat of roses in a still,
As that which from chafed musk cat's pores doth trill,
As the almighty balm of th' early east,
Such are the sweat drops of my mistress' breast.
And on her neck her skin such lustre sets,
They seem no sweat drops, but pearl carcanets.
Rank sweaty froth thy mistress' brow defiles,
Like spermatic issue of ripe menstruous boils,
Or like that scum, which, by need's lawless law
Enforced, Sanserra's starved men did draw
From parboiled shoes, and boots, and all the rest
Which were with any sovereign fatness blessed;
And like vile lying stones in saffroned tin,
Or warts, or weals, they hang upon her skin.
Round as the world's her head, on every side,
Like to the fatal ball which fell on Ide,
Or that whereof God had such jealousy,
As for the ravishing thereof we die.
Thy head is like a rough-hewn statue of jet,
Where marks for eyes, nose, mouth, are yet scarce set;
Like the first Chaos, or flat seeming face
Of Cynthia, when th' earth's shadows her embrace.
Like Proserpine's white beauty-keeping chest,
Or Jove's best fortune's urn, is her fair breast.
Thine's like worm-eaten trunks, clothed in seal's skin,
Or grave, that's dust without, and stink within.
And like that slender stalk, at whose end stands
The woodbine quivering, are her arms and hands.

Like rough-barked elm-boughs, or the russet skin
Of men late scourged for madness, or for sin,
Like sun-parched quarters on the city gate,
Such is thy tanned skin's lamentable state.
And like a bunch of ragged carrots stand
The short swollen fingers of thy gouty hand.
Then like the chemic's masculine equal fire,
Which in the limbec's warm womb doth inspire
Into th' earth's worthless dirt a soul of gold,
Such cherishing heat her best loved part doth hold.
Thine's like the dread mouth of a fired gun,
Or like hot liquid metals newly run
Into clay moulds, or like to that Etna
Where round about the grass is burnt away.
Are not your kisses then as filthy, and more,
As a worm sucking an envenomed sore?
Doth not thy fearful hand in feeling quake,
As one which gathering flowers, still fears a snake?
Is not your last act harsh, and violent,
As when a plough a stony ground doth rent?
So kiss good turtles, so devoutly nice
Are priests in handling reverent sacrifice,
And such in searching wounds the surgeon is
As we, when we embrace, or touch, or kiss.
Leave her, and I will leave comparing thus,
She and comparisons are odious.

ELEGY IX

The Autumnal

No spring, nor summer beauty hath such grace,
  As I have seen in one autumnal face.
Young beauties force our love, and that's a rape,
  This doth but counsel, yet you cannot scape.
If t'were a shame to love, here t'were no shame;
  Affection here takes reverence's name.
Were her first years the golden age? That's true,
  But now she's gold oft tried, and ever new.
That was her torrid and inflaming time,
  This is her tolerable tropic clime.
Faire eyes, who asks more heat than comes from hence,
  He in a fever wishes pestilence.
Call not these wrinkles, graves; if graves they were,
  They were Love's graves; for else he is no where.
Yet lies not Love dead here, but here doth sit
  Vow'd to this trench, like an anachorit.
And here, till hers, which must be his death, come,
  He doth not dig a grave, but build a tomb.
Here dwells he, though he sojourn ev'rywhere,
  In progress, yet his standing house is here.
Here where still evening is, not noon, nor night;
  Where no voluptuousness, yet all delight.
In all her words, unto all hearers fit,
  You may at revels, you at council, sit.
This is Love's timber, youth his underwood;
  There he, as wine in June, enrages blood,
Which then comes seasonabliest when our taste
  And appetite to other things is past.

Xerxes' strange Lydian love, the platan tree,
  Was lov'd for age, none being so large as she,
Or else because, being young, nature did bless
  Her youth with age's glory, barrenness.
If we love things long sought, age is a thing
  Which we are fifty years in compassing.
If transitory things, which soon decay,
  Age must be loveliest at the latest day.
But name not winter faces, whose skin's slack,
  Lank as an unthrift's purse, but a soul's sack;
Whose eyes seek light within, for all here's shade;
  Whose mouths are holes, rather worn out than made;
Whose every tooth to a several place is gone,
  To vex their souls at resurrection;
Name not these living death's-heads unto me,
  For these, not ancient, but antique be.
I hate extremes; yet I had rather stay
  With tombs than cradles, to wear out a day.
Since such love's natural lation is, may still
  My love descend, and journey down the hill,
Not panting after growing beauties, so,
  I shall ebb out with them, who homeward go.

ELEGY X

The Dream

Image of her whom I love, more than she,
  Whose fair impression in my faithful heart
Makes me her medal, and makes her love me,
  As kings do coins, to which their stamps impart
The value: go, and take my heart from hence,
  Which now is grown too great and good for me:
Honours oppress weak spirits, and our sense
  Strong objects dull; the more, the less we see.
When you are gone, and reason gone with you,
  Then fantasy is queen and soul, and all;
She can present joys meaner than you do,
  Convenient, and more proportional.
So, if I dream I have you, I have you,
  For all our joys are but fantastical.
And so I 'scape the pain, for pain is true;
  And sleep, which locks up sense, doth lock out all.
After a such fruition I shall wake,
  And, but the waking, nothing shall repent;
And shall to love more thankful sonnets make,
  Than if more honour, tears, and pains were spent.
But, dearest heart and dearer image, stay;
  Alas! true joys at best are dream enough;
Though you stay here, you pass too fast away:
  For even at first life's taper is a snuff.
Fill'd with her love, may I be rather grown
Mad with much heart, than idiot with none.

ELEGY XI

The Bracelet

Upon the loss of his mistress' chain, for which he made satisfaction.

Not that in colour it was like thy hair,
For armlets of that thou mayst let me wear;
Nor that thy hand it oft embrac'd and kiss'd,
For so it had that good, which oft I miss'd;
Nor for that silly old morality,
That, as these links were knit, our love should be;
Mourn I that I thy sevenfold chain have lost,
Nor for the luck sake; but the bitter cost.
O, shall twelve righteous angels, which as yet
No leaven of vile solder did admit;
Nor yet by any way have stray'd or gone
From the first state of their creation;
Angels, which heaven commanded to provide
All things to me, and be my faithful guide;
To gain new friends, to appease great enemies;
To comfort my soul, when I lie or rise;
Shall these twelve innocents, by thy severe
Sentence, dread judge, my sin's great burden bear?
Shall they be damn'd, and in the furnace thrown,
And punish'd for offences not their own?
They save not me, they do not ease my pains,
When in that hell they're burnt and tied in chains.
Were they but crowns of France, I carèd not,
For most of these, their country's natural rot,
I think, possesseth; they come here to us,
So pale, so lame, so lean, so ruinous.

And howsoe'er French kings most Christian be,
Their crowns are circumcis'd most Jewishly.
Or were they Spanish stamps, still travelling,
That are become as Catholic as their king,
Those unlick'd bear-whelps, unfiled pistolets
That—more than cannon shot—avails or lets;
Which, negligently left unrounded, look
Like many-angled figures in the book
Of some great conjurer that would enforce
Nature, as these do justice, from her course;
Which, as the soul quickens head, feet and heart,
As streams, like veins, run through th'earth's every part,
Visit all countries, and have slily made
Gorgeous France, ruin'd, ragged and decay'd;
Scotland, which knew no state, proud in one day,
And mangled seventeen-headed Belgia.
Or were it such gold as that wherewithal
Almighty chemics, from each mineral,
Having by subtle fire a soul out-pull'd;
Are dirtily and desperately gull'd:
I would not spit to quench the fire they're in,
For they are guilty of much heinous sin.
But shall my harmless angels perish? Shall
I lose my guard, my ease, my food, my all?
Much hope which they should nourish will be dead,
Much of my able youth, and lustihead
Will vanish; if thou love, let them alone,
For thou wilt love me less when they are gone;
And be content that some loud squeaking crier,
Well-pleas'd with one lean threadbare groat, for hire,
May like a devil roar through every street,
And gall the finder's conscience, if they meet.

Or let me creep to some dread conjurer,
That with fantastic schemes fills full much paper;
Which hath divided heaven in tenements,
And with whores, thieves, and murderers stuff'd his rents
So full, that though he pass them all in sin,
He leaves himself no room to enter in.
But if, when all his art and time is spent,
He say 'twill ne'er be found; yet be content;
Receive from him that doom ungrudgingly,
Because he is the mouth of destiny.
Thou say'st, alas! the gold doth still remain,
Though it be chang'd, and put into a chain;
So in the first fallen angels resteth still
Wisdom and knowledge; but 'tis turn'd to ill:
As these should do good works, and should provide
Necessities; but now must nurse thy pride.
And they are still bad angels; mine are none;
For form gives being, and their form is gone:
Pity these angels yet; their dignities
Pass Virtues, Powers, and Principalities.
But thou art resolute; thy will be done!
Yet with such anguish, as her only son
The mother in the hungry grave doth lay,
Unto the fire these martyrs I betray.
Good souls—for you give life to everything—
Good angels—for good messages you bring—
Destin'd you might have been to such an one,
As would have loved and worshipped you alone:
One that would suffer hunger, nakedness,
Yea death, ere he would make your number less;
But, I am guilty of your sad decay;
May your few fellows longer with me stay.

But O! thou wretched finder whom I hate
So, that I almost pity thy estate:
Gold being the heaviest metal amongst all,
May my most heavy curse upon thee fall:
Here fetter'd, manacled, and hang'd in chains,
First mayst thou bee; then chain'd to hellish pains;
Or be with foreign gold bribed to betray
Thy country, and fail both of it and thy pay.
May the next thing thou stoop'st to reach, contain
Poison, whose nimble fume rot thy moist brain;
Or libels, or some interdicted thing,
Which negligently kept, thy ruine bring.
Lust-bred diseases rot thee; and dwell with thee
Itching desire, and no ability.
May all the evils that gold ever wrought;
All mischief that all devils ever thought;
Want after plenty, poor and gouty age,
The plagues of travellers, love, marriage
Afflict thee, and at thy life's last moment,
May thy swollen sins themselves to thee present.
But, I forgive; repent thee honest man!
Gold is restorative, restore it then:
But if from it thou be'est loth to depart,
Because 'tis cordial, would 'twere at thy heart.

ELEGY XII

Come Fates; I fear you not! All whom I owe
Are paid, but you; then 'rest me ere I go.
But Chance from you all sovereignty hath got;
Love woundeth none but those whom Death dares not;
True if you were, and just in equity,
I should have vanquish'd her, as you did me;
Else lovers should not brave Death's pains, and live;
But 'tis a rule, 'Death comes not to relieve.'
Or, pale and wan Death's terrors, are they laid
So deep in lovers, they make Death afraid?
Or—the least comfort—have I company?
O'ercame she Fates, Love, Death, as well as me?
Yes, Fates do silk unto her distaff pay,
For ransom, which tax they on us do lay.
Love gives her youth—which is the reason why
Youths, for her sake, some wither and some die.
Poor Death can nothing give; yet, for her sake,
Still in her turn, he doth a lover take.
And if Death should prove false, she fears him not;
Our Muses, to redeem her, she hath got.
That fatal night we last kiss'd, I thus pray'd,
—Or rather, thus despair'd, I should have said—
Kisses, and yet despair! The forbid tree
Did promise (and deceive) no more than she.
Like lambs, that see their teats, and must eat hay,
A food, whose taste hath made me pine away.
Dives, when thou saw'st bliss, and craved'st to touch
A drop of water, thy great pains were such.
Here grief wants a fresh wit, for mine being spent,
And my sighs weary, groans are all my rent.

Unable longer to endure the pain,
They break like thunder, and do bring down rain.
Thus till dry tear solder my eye, I weep;
And then, I dream, how you securely sleep,
And in your dreams do laugh at me. I hate,
And pray Love all may; he pities my state,
But says, I therein no revenge shall find;
The sun would shine, though all the world were blind.
Yet, to try my hate, Love show'd me your tear;
And I had died, had not your smile been there.
Your frown undoes me; your smile is my wealth;
And as you please to look, I have my health.
Methought, Love pitying me, when he saw this,
Gave me your hands, the backs and palms to kiss.
That cured me not, but to bear pain gave strength;
And what is lost in force, is took in length.
I call'd on Love again, who fear'd you so,
That his compassion still proved greater woe;
For, then I dream'd I was in bed with you,
But durst not feel, for fear it should not be true.
This merits not your anger, had it been;
The queen of chastity was naked seen;
And in bed not to feel, the pain I took,
Was more than for Actæon not to look;
And that breast which lay ope, I did not know,
But for the clearness, from a lump of snow;
Nor that sweet teat which on the top it bore
From the rose-bud which for my sake you wore.
These griefs to issue forth, by verse I prove;
Or turn their course by travel and new love.
All would not do; the best at last I tried;
Unable longer to hold out, I died.

And then I found I lost life, death by flying;
Who hundreds live, are but so long in dying.
Charon did let me pass; I'll him requite.
To mark the groves or shades wrongs my delight;
I'll speak but of those ghosts I found alone,
Those thousand ghosts, whereof myself made one,
All images of thee; I asked them why?
The judge told me, all they for thee did die,
And therefore had for their Elysian bliss,
In one another their own loves to kiss.
O here I miss'd not bliss, but being dead ;
For lo! I dreamt, I dreamt, and waking said,
'Heaven, if who are in thee there must dwell,
How is't I now was there, and now I fell?'

ELEGY XIII

His Parting from Her

Since she must go, and I must mourn, come night,
Environ me with darkness, whilst I write:
Shadow that hell unto me, which alone
I am to suffer when my love is gone.
Alas! the darkest magic cannot do it,
Thou and great hell, to boot, are shadows to it.
Should Cynthia quit thee, Venus, and each star,
It would not form one thought dark as mine are.
I could lend thee obscureness now, and say
Out of my self, there should be no more day,
Such is already my self-want of sight,
Did not the fire within me force a light.
    O Love, that fire and darkness should be mixt,
Or to thy triumphs so strange torments fixt!
Is't because thou thyself art blind, that we
Thy martyrs must no more each other see?
Or tak'st thou pride to break us on the wheel,
And view old chaos in the pains we feel?
Or have we left undone some mutual rite,
That thus with parting thou seek'st us to spite?
No, no. The fault was mine, impute it me,
Or rather to conspiring destiny,
Which, since I lov'd for form before, decreed
That I should suffer when I lov'd indeed:
And therefore, sooner now than I can say,
I saw the golden fruit, 'tis rapt away.
Or as I had watched one drop in the vast stream,
And I left wealthy only in a dream.

Yet, Love, thou'rt blinder than myself in this,
To vex my dove-like friend for my amiss:
And where one sad truth may expiate
Thy wrath, to make her fortune run my fate.
So blinded Justice doth, when favourites fall,
Strike them, their house, their friends, their favourites all.
Was't not enough that thou didst dart thy fires
Into our bloods, inflaming our desires,
And made'st us sigh and blow, and pant, and burn,
And then thyself into our flames did'st turn?
Was't not enough, that thou didst hazard us
To paths in love so dark and dangerous:
And those so ambush'd round with household spies,
And over all, thy husband's tow'ring eyes
Inflam'd with th' ugly sweat of jealousy;
Yet went we not still on in constancy?
Have we for this guards, like spy on spy?
Had correspondence whilst the foe stood by?
Stol'n, more to sweeten them, our many blisses
Of meetings, conference, embracements, kisses?
Shadow'd with negligence our best respects?
Varied our language through all dialects
Of becks, winks, looks, and often under boards
Spoke dialogues with our feet far from our words?
Have we prov'd all these secrets of our art,
Yea, thy pale inwards, and thy panting heart?
And, after all this passed purgatory,
Must sad divorce make us the vulgar story?
First let our eyes be riveted quite through
Our turning brain, and both our lips grow to:
Let our arms clasp like ivy, and our fear
Freeze us together, that we may stick here,

Till Fortune, that would ruin us with the deed,
Strain her eyes open, and it make them bleed.
For Love it cannot be, whom hitherto
I have accus'd, should such a mischief do.

O Fortune, thou'rt not worth my least exclaim,
And plague enough thou hast in thy own name.
Do thy great worst; my friend and I have arms,
Though not against thy strokes, against thy harms.
Rend us in sunder; thou canst not divide
Our bodies so, but that our souls are tied,
And we can love by letters still and gifts,
And thoughts and dreams; love never wanteth shifts.
I will not look upon the quickening sun,
But straight her beauty to my sense shall run;
The air shall note her soft, the fire, most pure;
Water suggest her clear, and the earth sure.
Time shall not lose our passages; the spring,
How fresh our love was in the beginning;
The summer how it ripened in the ear;
And autumn, what our golden harvests were.
The winter I'll not think on to spite thee,
But count it a lost season; so shall she.

And dearest friend, since we must part, drown night
With hope of day—burthens well born are light—;
Though cold and darkness longer hang somewhere,
Yet Phoebus equally lights all the sphere.
And what he cannot in like portions pay,
The world enjoys in mass, and so we may.
Be then ever yourself, and let no woe
Win on your health, your youth, your beauty: so
Declare yourself base Fortune's enemy,
No less be your contempt than her inconstancy:

That I may grow enamoured on your mind,
When my own thoughts I there reflected find.
For this to th'comfort of my dear I vow,
My deeds shall still be what my words are now;
The poles shall move to teach me ere I start;
And when I change my love, I'll change my heart;
Nay, if I wax but cold in my desire,
Think, heaven hath motion lost, and the world, fire:
Much more I could, but many words have made
That oft suspected which men would persuade;
Take therefore all in this: I love so true,
As I will never look for less in you.

ELEGY XIV

Julia

Hark, news, O envy; thou shalt hear descried
My Julia; who as yet was ne'er envied.
To vomit gall in slander, swell her veins
With calumny, that hell itself disdains,
Is her continual practice; does her best,
To tear opinion e'en out of the breast
Of dearest friends, and—which is worse than vile—
Sticks jealousy in wedlock; her own child
Scapes not the showers of envy. To repeat
The monstrous fashions how, were alive to eat
Dear reputation; would to God she were
But half so loth to act vice, as to hear
My mild reproof. Lived Mantuan now again
That female Mastix to limn with his pen
This she Chimera that hath eyes of fire,
Burning with anger—anger feeds desire—
Tongued like the night crow, whose ill-boding cries
Give out for nothing but new injuries;
Her breath like to the juice in Taenarus,
That blasts the springs, though ne'er so prosperous;
Her hands, I know not how, used more to spill
The food of others than herself to fill;
But O! her mind, that Orcus, which includes
Legions of mischiefs, countless multitudes
Of formless curses, projects unmade up,
Abuses yet unfashion'd, thoughts corrupt,
Misshapen cavils, palpable untroths,
Inevitable errors, self-accusing loaths.

These, like those atoms swarming in the sun,
Throng in her bosom for creation.
I blush to give her half her due; yet say,
No poison's half so bad as Julia.

ELEGY XV

A Tale of a Citizen and His Wife

I sing no harm, good sooth, to any wight,
To lord or fool, cuckold, beggar or knight,
To peace-teaching lawyer, proctor or brave
Reformed or reducèd captain, knave,
Officer, juggler or justice of peace,
Juror or judge; I touch no fat sow's grease;
I am no libeller, nor will be any,
But—like a true man—say there are too many.
I fear not *ore tenus*; for my tale
Nor count nor counsellor will look red or pale.

   A citizen and his wife the other day
Both riding on one horse, upon the way
I overtook; the wench a pretty peat,
And—by her eye—well fitting for the feat.
I saw the lecherous citizen turn back
His head, and on his wife's lip steal a smack;
Whence apprehending that the man was kind,
Riding before to kiss his wife behind,
To get acquaintance with him I began
To sort discourse fit for so fine a man:
I ask'd the number of the plaguing bill;
Ask'd if the custom farmers held out still;
Of the Virginian plot, and whether Ward
The traffic of the island seas had marr'd;
Whether the Britain Burse did fill apace,
And likely were to give th' Exchange disgrace.

Of new-built Aldgate, and the Moor-field crosses,
Of store of bankrupts, and poor merchants' losses
I urgèd him to speak; but he—as mute
As an old courtier worn to his last suit—
Replies with only yeas and nays; at last
—To fit his element—my theme I cast
On tradesmen's gains; that set his tongue a-going.
'Alas! good sir,' quoth he, 'There is no doing
In court or city now'; she smiled, and I,
And, in my conscience, both gave him the lie
In one met thought; but he went on apace,
And at the present time with such a face
He rail'd, as fray'd me; for he gave no praise
To any but my Lord of Essex' days;
Call'd that the age of action—'True!' quoth I—
'There's now as great an itch of bravery,
And heat of taking up, but cold lay down,
For, put to push of pay, away they run;
Our only city trades of hope now are
Bawd, tavern-keepers, whores, and scriveners.
The much of privileged kinsmen and store
Of fresh protections make the rest all poor.
In the first state of their creation
Though many stoutly stand, yet proves not one
A righteous pay-master.' Thus ran he on
In a continued rage; so void of reason
Seem'd his harsh talk, I sweat for fear of treason.
And—troth—how could I less? when in the prayer
For the protection of the wise Lord Mayor,
And his wise brethren's worships, when one prayeth,
He swore that none could say amen with faith.
To get off him from what I glow'd to hear,

In happy time an angel did appear,
The bright sign of a loved and well-tried inn,
Where many citizens with their wives had been
Well used and often; here I pray'd him stay,
To take some due refreshment by the way.
Look, how he look'd that hid the gold, his hope,
And at return found nothing but a rope,
So he at me; refused and made away,
Though willing she pleaded a weary stay.
I found my miss, struck hands, and pray'd him tell—
To hold acquaintance still—where he did dwell.
He barely named the street, promised the wine,
But his kind wife gave me the very sign.

ELEGY XVI

The Expostulation

To make the doubt clear, that no woman's true,
Was it my fate to prove it strong in you?
Thought I, but one had breathèd purest air;
And must she needs be false, because she's fair?
Is it your beauty's mark, or of your youth,
Or your perfection, not to study truth?
Or think you heaven is deaf, or hath no eyes?
Or those it hath smile at your perjuries?
Are vows so cheap with women, or the matter
Whereof they're made, that they are writ in water,
And blown away with wind? Or doth their breath,
Both hot and cold, at once make life and death?
Who could have thought so many accents sweet
Form'd into words, so may sighs should meet
As from our hearts, so many oaths, and tears
Sprinkled among, all sweeten'd by our fears,
And the divine impression of stolen kisses,
That seal'd the rest, should now prove empty blisses?
Did you draw bonds to forfeit? sign to break?
Or must we read you quite from what you speak,
And find the truth out the wrong way? or must
He first desire you false, would wish you just?
O! I profane! though most of women be
This kind of beast, my thoughts shall except thee,
My dearest love; though froward jealousy
With circumstance might urge thy inconstancy,
Sooner I'll think the sun will cease to cheer
The teeming earth, and that forget to bear;

Sooner that rivers will run back, or Thames
With ribs of ice in June will bind his streams ;
Or nature, by whose strength the world endures,
Would change her course, before you alter yours.
But O! that treacherous breast, to whom weak you
Did drift our counsels, and we both may rue,
Having his falsehood found too late ; 'twas he
That made me cast you guilty, and you me ;
Whilst he, black wretch, betray'd each simple word
We spake, unto the cunning of a third.
Cursed may he be, that so our love hath slain,
And wander on the earth, wretched as Cain,
Wretched as he, and not deserve least pity.
In plaguing him, let misery by witty;
Let all eyes shun him, and he shun each eye,
'Til he be noisome as his infamy ;
May he without remorse deny God thrice,
And not be trusted more on his soul's price;
And, after all self-torment, when he dies,
May wolves tear out his heart, vultures his eyes,
Swine eat his bowels, and his falser tongue
That utter'd all, be to some raven flung;
And let his carrion corse be a longer feast
To the king's dogs, than any other beast.
Now have I cursed, let us our love revive;
In me the flame was never more alive.
I could begin again to court and praise,
And in that pleasure lengthen the short days
Of my life's lease; like painters that do take
Delight, not in made work, but whiles they make.
I could renew those times, when first I saw
Love in your eyes, that gave my tongue the law

To like what you liked; and at masks and plays
Commend the self-same actors, the same ways;
Ask how you did, and often with intent
Of being officious, be impertinent;
All which were such soft pastimes, as in these
Love was as subtly catch'd as a disease.
But being got, it is a treasure sweet,
Which to defend is harder than to get;
And ought not be profaned, on either part,
For though 'tis got by chance, 'tis kept by art.

ELEGY XVII

On His Mistress

By our first strange and fatal interview,
By all desires which thereof did ensue,
By our long starving hopes, by that remorse
Which my words masculine persuasive force
Begot in thee, and by the memory
Of hurts, which spies and rivals threaten'd me,
I calmly beg. But by thy father's wrath,
By all pains, which want and divorcement hath,
I conjure thee, and all the oaths which I
And thou have sworn to seal joint constancy,
Here I unswear, and overswear them thus ;
Thou shalt not love by ways so dangerous.
Temper, O fair love, love's impetuous rage;
Be my true mistress still, not my feign'd page.
I'll go, and, by thy kind leave, leave behind
Thee, only worthy to nurse in my mind
Thirst to come back; O! if thou die before,
My soul from other lands to thee shall soar.
Thy else almighty beauty cannot move
Rage from the seas, nor thy love teach them love,
Nor tame wild Boreas' harshness; thou hast read
How roughly he in pieces shivered
Fair Orithea, whom he swore he loved.
Fall ill or good, 'tis madness to have proved
Dangers unurged; feed on this flattery,
That absent lovers one in th' other be.
Dissemble nothing, not a boy, nor change
Thy body's habit, nor mind; be not strange

To thyself only. All will spy in thy face
A blushing womanly discovering grace.
Richly clothed apes are call'd apes, and as soon
Eclipsed as bright, we call the moon the moon.
Men of France, changeable chameleons,
Spitals of diseases, shops of fashions,
Love's fuellers, and the rightest company
Of players, which upon the world's stage be,
Will quickly know thee, and no less, alas!
Th' indifferent Italian, as we pass
His warm land, well content to think thee page,
Will hunt thee with such lust, and hideous rage,
As Lot's fair guests were vex'd. But none of these
Nor spongy hydroptic Dutch shall thee displease,
If thou stay here. O stay here, for, for thee
England is only a worthy gallery,
To walk in expectation, till from thence
Our greatest king call thee to his presence.
When I am gone, dream me some happiness;
Nor let thy looks our long-hid love confess;
Nor praise, nor dispraise me, nor bless nor curse
Openly love's force, nor in bed fright thy nurse
With midnight's startings, crying out, O! O!
Nurse, O! my love is slain ; I saw him go
O'er the white Alps alone ; I saw him, I,
Assail'd, fight, taken, stabb'd, bleed, fall, and die.
Augur me better chance, except dread Jove
Think it enough for me to have had thy love.

ELEGY XVIII

Variety

The heavens rejoice in motion; why should I
Abjure my so much loved variety,
And not with many youth and love divide?
Pleasure is none, if not diversified.
The sun that, sitting in the chair of light,
Sheds flame into what else so ever doth seem bright,
Is not contented at one sign to inn,
But ends his year, and with a new begin.
All things do willingly in change delight,
The fruitful mother of our appetite;
Rivers the clearer and more pleasing are,
Where their fair-spreading streams run wide and clear;
And a dead lake, that no strange bark doth greet,
Corrupts itself, and what doth live in it.
Let no man tell me such a one is fair,
And worthy all alone my love to share.
Nature in her hath done the liberal part
Of a kind mistress, and employed her art
To make her lovable, and I aver
Him not humane, that would turn back from her.
I love her well, and would, if need were, die,
To do her service. But follows it that I
Must serve her only, when I may have choice?
The law is hard, and shall not have my voice.
The last I saw in all extremes is fair,
And holds me in the sunbeams of her hair;
Her nymph-like features such agreements have,
That I could venture with her to the grave.

Another's brown; I like her not the worse;
Her tongue is soft and takes me with discourse.
Others, for that they well descended were,
Do in my love obtain as large a share;
And though they be not fair, 'tis much with me
To win their love only for their degree.
And though I fail of my required ends,
The attempt is glorious and itself commends.
How happy were our sires in ancient time,
Who held plurality of loves no crime.
With them it was accounted charity
To stir up race of all indifferently;
Kindred were not exempted from the bands,
Which with the Persian still in usage stands.
Women were then no sooner ask'd than won,
And what they did was honest and well done.
But since this little Honour hath been used,
Our weak credulity hath been abused;
The golden laws of nature are repeal'd,
Which our first fathers in such reverence held;
Our liberty reversed and charters gone;
And we made servants to Opinion;
A monster in no certain shape attired,
And whose original is much desired,
Formless at first, but growing on its fashions,
And doth prescribe manners and laws to nations.
Here love received immedicable harms,
And was despoiled of his daring arms;
A greater want than is his daring eyes,
He lost those awful wings with which he flies,
His sinewy bow and those immortal darts,
With which he is wont to bruise resisting hearts.

Only some few, strong in themselves and free,
Retain the seeds of ancient liberty,
Following that part of love although depress'd,
Yet make a throne for him within their breast,
In spite of modern censures him avowing
Their sovereign, all service him allowing.
Amongst which troop although I am the least,
Yet equal in perfection with the best,
I glory in subjection of his hand,
Nor ever did decline his least command;
For in whatever form the message came
My heart did open and receive the same,
But time will in his course a point descry
When I this lovèd service must deny;
For our allegiance temporary is;
With firmer age returns our liberties.
What time in years and judgement we reposed,
Shall not so easily be to change disposed,
Nor to the art of several eyes obeying,
But beauty with true worth securely weighing;
Which being found assembled in some one
We'll love her ever, and love her alone.

ELEGY XIX

Love's Progress

Whoever loves, if he do not propose
The right true end of love, he's one that goes
To sea for nothing but to make him sick.
Love is a bear-whelp born : if we o'er-lick
Our love, and force it new strange shapes to take,
We err, and of a lump a monster make.
Were not a calf a monster, that were grown
Faced like a man, though better than his own?
Perfection is in unity ; prefer
One woman first, and then one thing in her.
I, when I value gold, may think upon
The ductileness, the application,
The wholesomeness, the ingenuity,
From rust, from soil, from fire ever free;
But if I love it, 'tis because 'tis made
By our new nature, use, the soul of trade.
    All this in women we might think upon—
If women had them—and yet love but one.
Can men more injure women than to say
They love them for that, by which they are not they?
Makes virtue woman? must I cool my blood
Till I both be, and find one wise and good?
May barren angels love so. But if we
Make love to woman, virtue is not she,
As beauty's not, nor wealth. He that strays thus
From her to hers is more adulterous
Than if he took her maid. Search every sphere
And firmament, our Cupid is not there.

He's an infernal god, and underground
With Pluto dwells, where gold and fire abound.
Men to such gods their sacrificing coals
Did not on altars lay, but pits and holes.
Although we see celestial bodies move
Above the earth, the earth we till and love.
So we her airs contemplate, words and heart,
And virtues; but we love the centric part.

    Nor is the soul more worthy, or more fit
For love, than this, as infinite as it.
But in attaining this desired place
How much they err, that set out at the face?
The hair a forest is of ambushes,
Of springs, snares, fetters and manacles;
The brow becalms us when 'tis smooth and plain,
And when 'tis wrinkled, shipwrecks us again;
Smooth, 'tis a paradise, where we would have
Immortal stay, but wrinkled 'tis a grave.
The nose, like to the first meridian, runs
Not 'twixt an east and west, but 'twixt two suns;
It leaves a cheek, a rosy hemisphere,
On either side, and then directs us where
Upon the islands fortunate we fall,
(Not faint Canaries, but ambrosial),
Her swelling lips, to which when we are come,
We anchor there, and think ourselves at home,
For they seem all ; there Sirens' songs and there
Wise Delphic oracles do fill the ear.
There, in a creek where chosen pearls do swell,
The remora, her cleaving tongue, doth dwell.
These and the glorious promontory, her chin,
O'erpast, and the straight Hellespont between

The Sestos and Abydos of her breasts,
Not of two lovers, but two loves, the nests,
Succeeds a boundless sea, but yet thine eye
Some island moles may scattered there descry;
And sailing towards her India, in that way
Shall at her fair Atlantic navel stay.
Though there the current be the pilot made,
Yet ere thou be where thou shouldst be embay'd,
Thou shalt upon another forest set,
Where many shipwreck, and no further get.
When thou art there, consider what this chase
Misspent by thy beginning at the face.
    Rather set out below; practise thy art;
Some symmetry the foot hath with that part
Which thou dost seek, and is thy map for that,
Lovely enough to stop, but not stay at.
Least subject to disguise and change it is;
Men say the devil never can change his;
It is the emblem that hath figured
Firmness; 'tis the first part that comes to bed.
Civility we see refined; the kiss,
Which at the face began, transplanted is,
Since to the hand, since to the imperial knee,
Now at the papal foot delights to be.
If kings think that the nearer way, and do
Rise from the foot, lovers may do so too;
For as free spheres move faster far than can
Birds, whom the air resists, so may that man
Which goes this empty and ethereal way,
Than if at beauty's elements he stay.
Rich Nature in women wisely made
Two purses, and their mouths aversely laid.

They then which to the lower tribute owe,
That way which that exchequer looks must go;
He which doth not, his error is as great,
As who by clyster gives the stomach meat.

ELEGY XX

To His Mistress, Going to Bed

Come, Madam, come, all rest my powers defy,
Until I labour, I in labour lie.
The foe oft-times having the foe in sight,
Is tir'd with standing though he never fight.
Off with that girdle, like heaven's zone glistering,
But a far fairer world encompassing.
Unpin that spangled breastplate which you wear,
That th'eyes of busy fools may be stopped there.
Unlace yourself, for that harmonious chime,
Tells me from you, that now it is bed time.
Off with that happy busk, which I envy,
That still can be, and still can stand so nigh.
Your gown going off, such beauteous state reveals,
As when from flowery meads th'hill's shadow steals.
Off with that wiry coronet and shew
The hairy diadem which on you doth grow:
Off with your hose and shoes; then softly tread
In this love's hallow'd temple, this soft bed.
In such white robes, heaven's angels used to be
Received by men; thou angel bring'st with thee
A heaven like Mahomet's paradise; and though
Ill spirits walk in white, we easily know,
By this these angels from an evil sprite,
Those set our hairs, but these our flesh upright.
    Licence my roving hands, and let them go,
Before, behind, between, above, below.
O my America! my new-found-land,
My kingdom, safeliest when with one man mann'd,

My mine of precious stones, my Empirie,
How blest am I in this discovering thee!
To enter in these bonds, is to be free;
Then where my hand is set, my seal shall be.
    Full nakedness! All joys are due to thee,
As souls unbodied, bodies uncloth'd must be,
To taste whole joys. Gems which you women use
Are like Atlanta's balls, cast in men's views,
That when a fool's eye lighteth on a gem,
His earthly soul may covet theirs, not them.
Like pictures, or like books' gay coverings made
For laymen, are all women thus array'd;
Themselves are mystic books, which only we
(Whom their imputed grace will dignify)
Must see reveal'd. Then since that I may know;
As liberally, as to a midwife, shew
Thyself: cast all, yea, this white linen hence,
There is no penance due to innocence.
    To teach thee, I am naked first; why then
What needst thou have more covering than a man.

SECTION III:
EPITHALAMIA OR
MARRIAGE SONGS

An Epithalamion or Marriage Song on the Lady Elizabeth and Count Palatine, being married on St. Valentine's Day

I

Hail Bishop Valentine, whose day this is;
    All the air is thy diocese,
    And all the chirping choristers
And other birds are thy parishioners;
    Thou marriest every year
The lyric lark, and the grave whispering dove,
The sparrow that neglects his life for love,
The household bird with the red stomacher;
    Thou mak'st the blackbird speed as soon,
As doth the goldfinch, or the halcyon ;
The husband cock looks out, and straight is sped,
And meets his wife, which brings her feather-bed.
This day more cheerfully than ever shine;
This day, which might enflame thyself, old Valentine.

II

Till now, thou warmd'st with multiplying loves
    Two larks, two sparrows, or two doves;
    All that is nothing unto this;
For thou this day couplest two phoenixes;
    Thou mak'st a taper see
What the sun never saw, and what the Ark
—Which was of fouls and beasts the cage and park—
Did not contain, one bed contains, through thee;

Two phoenixes, whose joined breasts
Are unto one another mutual nests,
Where motion kindles such fires as shall give
Young phoenixes, and yet the old shall live;
Whose love and courage never shall decline,
But make the whole year through, thy day, O Valentine.

III

Up then, fair phoenix bride, frustrate the sun;
     Thyself from thine affection
     Takest warmth enough, and from thine eye
All lesser birds will take their jollity.
      Up, up, fair bride, and call
Thy stars from out their several boxes, take
Thy rubies, pearls, and diamonds forth, and make
Thyself a constellation of them all;
     And by their blazing signify
That a great princess falls, but doth not die.
Be thou a new star, that to us portends
Ends of much wonder; and be thou those ends.
Since thou dost this day in new glory shine,
May all men date records from this day, Valentine.

IV

Come forth, come forth, and as one glorious flame
     Meeting another grows the same,
     So meet thy Frederick, and so
To an inseparable union go,

> Since separation
Falls not on such things as are infinite,
Nor things, which are but one, can disunite.
You're twice inseparable, great, and one;
> Go then to where the bishop stays,
To make you one, his way, which divers ways
Must be effected; and when all is past,
And that you're one, by hearts and hands made fast,
You two have one way left, yourselves to entwine,
Besides this bishop's knot, of Bishop Valentine.

V

But O, what ails the sun, that here he stays,
> Longer today than other days?
> Stays he new light from these to get?
And finding here such stars, is loth to set?
> And why do you two walk,
So slowly paced in this procession?
Is all your care but to be look'd upon,
And be to others spectacle, and talk?
> The feast with gluttonous delays
Is eaten, and too long their meat they praise;
The masquers come late, and I think, will stay,
Like fairies, till the cock crow them away.
Alas! did not antiquity assign
A night as well as day, to thee, old Valentine?

VI

They did, and night is come; and yet we see
  Formalities retarding thee.
  What mean these ladies, which—as though
They were to take a clock in pieces—go
  So nicely about the bride?
A bride, before a 'Good-night' could be said,
Should vanish from her clothes into her bed,
As souls from bodies steal, and are not spied.
  But now she's laid; what though she be?
Yet there are more delays, for where is he?
He comes and passes through sphere after sphere;
First her sheets, then her arms, then anywhere.
Let not this day, then, but this night be thine;
Thy day was but the eve to this, O Valentine.

VII

Here lies a she sun, and a he moon there;
  She gives the best light to his sphere ;
  Or each is both, and all, and so
They unto one another nothing owe;
  And yet they do, but are
So just and rich in that coin which they pay,
That neither would, nor needs forbear, nor stay;
Neither desires to be spared, nor to spare.
  They quickly pay their debt, and then
Take no acquittances, but pay again;
They pay, they give, they lend, and so let fall
No such occasion to be liberal.

More truth, more courage in these two do shine,
Than all thy turtles have, and sparrows, Valentine.

VIII

And by this act of these two phoenixes
    Nature again restorèd is;
    For since these two are two no more,
There's but one phoenix still, as was before.
    Rest now at last, and we—
As satyrs watch the sun's uprise—will stay
Waiting when your eyes opened let out day,
Only desired because your face we see.
    Others near you shall whispering speak,
And wagers lay, at which side day will break,
And win by observing, then, whose hand it is
That opens first a curtain, hers or his:
This will be tried tomorrow after nine,
Till which hour, we thy day enlarge, O Valentine.

Epithalamion made at Lincoln's Inn

Hail sun-beams in the east are spread;
Leave, leave, fair bride, your solitary bed;
   No more shall you return to it alone;
It nurseth sadness, and your body's print,
Like to a grave, the yielding down doth dint;
   You, and your other you, meet there anon.
   Put forth, put forth, that warm balm-breathing thigh,
Which when next time you in these sheets will smother,
   There it must meet another,
     Which never was, but must be, oft, more nigh.
Come glad from thence, go gladder than you came;
Today put on perfection, and a woman's name.

Daughters of London, you which be
Our golden mines, and furnish'd treasury;
   You which are angels, yet still bring with you
Thousands of angels on your marriage days;
Help with your presence, and devise to praise
   These rites, which also unto you grow due;
   Conceitedly dress her, and be assign'd,
By you fit place for every flower and jewel;
   Make her for love fit fuel,
     As gay as Flora and as rich as Ind;
So may she, fair and rich in nothing lame,
Today put on perfection, and a woman's name.

And you frolic patricians,
Sons of those senators, wealth's deep oceans;
   Ye painted courtiers, barrels of other's wits;
Ye countrymen, who but your beasts love none;

Ye of those fellowships, whereof he's one,
    Of study and play made strange hermaphrodites,
    Here shine; this bridegroom to the temple bring.
Lo, in yon path which store of strew'd flowers graceth,
    The sober virgin paceth;
        Except my sight fail, 'tis no other thing.
Weep not, nor blush, here is no grief nor shame,
Today put on perfection, and a woman's name.

Thy two-leaved gates, fair temple, unfold,
And these two in thy sacred bosom hold,
    Till mystically join'd but one they be;
Then may thy lean and hunger-starvèd womb
Long time expect their bodies, and their tomb,
    Long after their own parents fatten thee.
    All elder claims, and all cold barrenness,
All yielding to new loves, be far for ever,
    Which might these two dissever;
        Always, all th'other may each one possess;
For the best bride, best worthy of praise and fame,
Today puts on perfection, and a woman's name.

Winter days bring much delight,
Not for themselves, but for they soon bring night;
    Other sweets wait thee than these diverse meats,
Other disports than dancing jollities,
Other love-tricks than glancing with the eyes,
    But that the sun still in our half sphere sweats;
He flies in winter, but he now stands still.
Yet shadows turn; noon point he hath attain'd;
    His steeds will be restrain'd,
        But gallop lively down the western hill.

Thou shalt, when he hath run the heaven's half frame,
Tonight put on perfection, and a woman's name.

The amorous evening star is rose,
Why then should not our amorous star inclose
    Herself in her wish'd bed? Release your strings,
Musicians; and dancers take some truce
With these your pleasing labours, for great use
    As much weariness as perfection brings.
    You, and not only you, but all toil'd beasts
Rest duly; at night all their toils are dispensed;
    But in their beds commenced
        Are other labours, and more dainty feasts.
She goes a maid, who, lest she turn the same,
Tonight puts on perfection, and a woman's name.

Thy virgin's girdle now untie,
And in thy nuptial bed, love's altar, lie
    A pleasing sacrifice; now dispossess
Thee of these chains and robes, which were put on
To adorn the day, not thee; for thou, alone,
    Like virtue and truth, art best in nakedness.
    This bed is only to virginity
A grave, but to a better state, a cradle.
    Till now thou wast but able
        To be, what now thou art; then, that by thee
No more be said, 'I may be,' but, 'I am,'
Tonight put on perfection, and a woman's name.

Even like a faithful man content,
That this life for a better should be spent,
    So she a mother's rich style doth prefer,

And at the bridegroom's wish'd approach doth lie,
Like an appointed lamb, when tenderly
    The priest comes on his knees to embowel her.
    Now sleep or watch with more joy; and, O light
Of heaven, tomorrow rise thou hot, and early;
    This sun will love so dearly
        Her rest, that long, long we shall want her sight.
Wonders are wrought, for she, which had no maim,
Tonight puts on perfection, and a woman's name.

Eclogue: 1613, December 26

Allophanes finding Idios in the country in Christmas time, reprehends his
absence from court, at the marriage of the Earl of Somerset; Idios gives an
account of his purpose therein, and of his actions there.

ALLOPHANES
Unseasonable man, statue of ice,
What could to country's solitude entice
Thee, in this year's cold and decrepit time?
Nature's instinct draws to the warmer clime
Even smaller birds, who by that courage dare
In numerous fleets sail through their sea, the air.
What delicacy can in fields appear,
Whilst Flora herself doth a frieze jerkin wear?
Whilst winds do all the trees and hedges strip
Of leaves, to furnish rods enough to whip
Thy madness from thee, and all springs by frost
Have taken cold, and their sweet murmurs lost?
If thou thy faults or fortunes wouldst lament
With just solemnity, do it in Lent.
At court the spring already advanced is,
The sun stays longer up; and yet not his
The glory is; far other, other fires.
First, zeal to prince and state, then love's desires
Burn in one breast, and like heaven's two great lights,
The first doth govern days, the other, nights.
And then that early light which did appear
Before the sun and moon created were,
The princes favour, is diffused o'er all,
From which all fortunes, names, and natures fall.

Then from those wombs of stars, the bride's bright eyes,
At every glance, a constellation flies,
And sows the court with stars, and doth prevent
In light and power, the all-eyed firmament.
First her eyes kindle other ladies' eyes,
Then from their beams their jewels' lustres rise,
And from their jewels torches do take fire,
And all is warmth, and light, and good desire.
Most other courts, alas! are like to hell,
Where in dark places, fire without light doth dwell;
Or but like stoves; for lust and envy get
Continual, but artificial heat.
Here zeal and love grown one all clouds digest,
And make our court an everlasting east.
And canst thou be from thence?

  IDIOS   No, I am there;
As heaven—to men disposed—is everywhere,
So are those courts, whose princes animate
Not only all their house but all their state.
Let no man think, because he's full, he hath all.
Kings—as their pattern, God—are liberal
Not only in fullness, but capacity,
Enlarging narrow men to feel and see,
And comprehend the blessings they bestow.
So, reclused hermits oftentimes do know
More of heaven's glory than a worldling can.
As man is of the world, the heart of man
Is an epitome of God's great book
Of creatures, and man need no farther look;
So is the country of courts, where sweet peace doth,

As their own common soul, give life to both;
And am I then from court?

  ALLOPHANES   Dreamer, thou art:
Think'st thou, fantastic, that thou hast a part
In the Indian fleet, because thou hast
A little spice or amber in thy taste?
Because thou art not frozen, art thou warm?
Seest thou all good, because thou seest no harm?
The earth doth in her inner bowels hold
Stuff well-disposed, and which would fain be gold;
But never shall, except it chance to lie
So upward, that heaven gild it with his eye.
As, for divine things, faith comes from above,
So, for best civil use, all tinctures move
From higher powers; from God religion springs,
Wisdom and honour from the use of kings:
Then unbeguile thyself, and know with me,
That angels, though on earth employ'd they be,
Are still in heaven, so he is still at home
That doth abroad to honest actions come.
Chide thyself then, O fool, which yesterday
Mightst have read more than all thy books bewray;
Hast thou a history, which doth present
A court, where all affections do assent
Unto the king's, and that that king's are just;
And where it is no levity to trust;
Where there is no ambition, but to obey;
Where men need whisper nothing, and yet may;
Where the king's favours are so placed, that all
Find that the king therein is liberal

To them, in him, because his favours bend
To virtue, to the which they all pretend?
Thou hast no such; yet here was this, and more.
An earnest lover, wise then, and before,
Our little Cupid hath sued livery,
And is no more in his minority;
He is admitted now into that breast
Where the king's counsels and his secrets rest.
What hast thou lost, O ignorant man?

IDIOS   I knew
All this, and only therefore I withdrew.
To know and feel all this, and not to have
Words to express it, makes a man a grave
Of his own thoughts; I would not therefore stay
At a great feast, having no grace to say.
And yet I 'scaped not here; for being come
Full of the common joy, I utter'd some.
Read then this nuptial song, which was not made
Either the court or men's hearts to invade;
But since I'm dead and buried, I could frame
No epitaph, which might advance my fame
So much as this poor song, which testifies
I did unto that day some sacrifice.

I

The time of the marriage
Thou art reprieved, old year, thou shalt not die;
    Though thou upon thy death-bed lie,
    And should'st within five days expire,

Yet thou art rescued by a mightier fire
    Than thy old soul, the sun,
When he doth in his largest circle run.
The passage of the west or east would thaw,
And open wide their easy liquid jaw
To all our ships, could a Promethean art
Either unto the northern pole impart
The fire of these inflaming eyes, or of this loving heart.

II
Equality of persons

But undiscerning Muse, which heart, which eyes,
    In this new couple, dost thou prize,
    When his eye as inflaming is
As hers, and her heart loves as well as his?
    Be tried by beauty, and then
The bridegroom is a maid, and not a man;
If by that manly courage they be tried,
Which scorns unjust opinion; then the bride
Becomes a man. Should chance or envy's art
Divide these two, whom nature scarce did part,
Since both have the inflaming eye, and both the
        loving heart?

III
Raising of the bridegroom

Though it be some divorce to think of you
    Single, so much one are you two,
    Let me here contemplate thee,
First, cheerful bridegroom, and first let me see,

How thou prevent'st the sun,
And his red foaming horses dost outrun;
How, having laid down in thy Sovereign's breast
All businesses, from thence to reinvest
Them when these triumphs cease, thou forward art
To show to her, who doth the like impart,
The fire of thy inflaming eyes, and of thy loving heart.

IV
Raising of the bride

But now to thee, fair bride, it is some wrong,
  To think thou wert in bed so long.
  Since soon thou liest down first, 'tis fit
Thou in first rising shouldst allow for it.
  Powder thy radiant hair,
Which if without such ashes thou wouldst wear,
Thou which, to all which come to look upon,
Wert meant for Phoebus, wouldst be Phaëton.
For our ease, give thine eyes th' unusual part
Of joy, a tear; so quench'd, thou mayst impart,
To us that come, thy inflaming eyes; to him, thy
    loving heart.

V
Her apparelling

Thus thou descend'st to our infirmity,
  Who can the sun in water see.
  So dost thou, when in silk and gold
Thou cloud'st thyself; since we which do behold
  Are dust and worms, 'tis just,

Our objects be the fruits of worms and dust.
Let every jewel be a glorious star,
Yet stars are not so pure as their spheres are;
And though thou stoop, to appear to us, in part,
Still in that picture thou entirely art,
Which thy inflaming eyes have made within his
     loving heart.

VI

Going to the chapel

Now from your easts you issue forth, and we,
    As men, which through a cypress see
    The rising sun, do think it two;
So, as you go to church, do think of you;
    But that veil being gone,
By the church rites you are from thenceforth one.
The church triumphant made this match before,
And now the militant doth strive no more.
Then, reverend priest, who God's Recorder art,
Do, from his dictates, to these two impart
All blessings which are seen, or thought, by angel's
    eye or heart.

VII

The benediction

Blest pair of swans, O may you interbring
    Daily new joys, and never sing;
    Live, till all grounds of wishes fail,
Till honour, yea, till wisdom grow so stale,
    That new great heights to try,

It must serve your ambition, to die;
Raise heirs, and may here, to the world's end, live
Heirs from this king, to take thanks, you, to give.
Nature and grace do all, and nothing art;
May never age or error overthwart
With any west these radiant eyes, with any north this
      heart.

VIII

Feasts and revels

But you are over-blessed. Plenty this day
    Injures; it causeth time to stay;
    The tables groan, as though this feast
Would, as the flood, destroy all fowl and beast.
    And were the doctrine new
That the earth moved, this day would make it true;
For every part to dance and revel goes,
They tread the air, and fall not where they rose.
Though six hours since the sun to bed did part,
The masks and banquets will not yet impart
A sunset to these weary eyes, a centre to this heart.

IX

The bride's going to bed

What mean'st thou, bride, this company to keep?
    To sit up, till thou fain wouldst sleep?
    Thou mayst not, when thou'rt laid, do so;
Thyself must to him a new banquet grow;
    And you must entertain
And do all this day's dances o'er again.

Know that if sun and moon together do
Rise in one point, they do not set so too.
Therefore thou mayst, fair bride, to bed depart;
Thou art not gone, being gone; where'er thou art,
  Thou leavest in him thy watchful eyes, in him thy
      loving heart.

X
The bridegroom's coming

As he that sees a star fall, runs apace,
    And finds a jelly in the place,
      So doth the bridegroom haste as much,
Being told this star is fallen, and finds her such.
    And as friends may look strange,
    By a new fashion, or apparel's change,
Their souls, though long acquainted they had been,
These clothes, their bodies, never yet had seen.
Therefore at first she modestly might start,
But must forthwith surrender every part,
As freely as each to each before gave either eye or
      heart.

XI
The good-night

Now, as in Tullia's tomb, one lamp burnt clear,
    Unchanged for fifteen hundred year,
      May these love-lamps we here enshrine,
In warmth, light, lasting, equal the divine.
    Fire ever doth aspire,
And makes all like itself, turns all to fire,

But ends in ashes; which these cannot do,
For none of these is fuel, but fire too.
This is joy's bonfire, then, where love's strong arts
Make of so noble individual parts
One fire of four inflaming eyes, and of two loving
      hearts.

IDIOS As I have brought this song, that I may do
A perfect sacrifice, I'll burn it too.

ALLOPHANES No, sir. This paper I have justly got,
For, in burnt incense, the perfume is not
His only that presents it, but of all;
Whatever celebrates this festival
Is common, since the joy thereof is so.
Nor may yourself be priest; but let me go
Back to the court, and I will lay it upon
Such altars, as prize your devotion.

SECTION IV:
SATIRES

SATIRE I

Away thou fondling motely humourist,
Leave me, and in this standing wooden chest,
Consorted with these few books, let me lie
In prison, and here be coffin'd, when I die;
Here are God's conduits, grave divines; and here
Nature's secretary, the Philosopher;
And jolly statesmen, which teach how to tie
The sinews of a city's mystic body;
Here gathering chroniclers, and by them stand
Giddy fantastic poets of each land.
Shall I leave all this constant company,
And follow headlong, wild uncertain thee?
First swear by thy best love in earnest
—If thou which lov'st all, canst love any best—
Thou wilt not leave me in the middle street,
Though some more spruce companion thou dost meet,
Not though a captain do come in thy way
Bright parcel gilt, with forty dead men's pay,
Nor though a brisk perfum'd pert courtier
Deign with a nod, thy courtesy to answer.
Nor come a velvet justice with a long
Great train of blue coats, twelve, or fourteen strong,
Wilt thou grin or fawn on him, or prepare
A speech to court his beauteous son and heir.
For better or worse take me, or leave me:
To take and leave me is adultery.
O monstrous, superstitious puritan,
Of refin'd manners, yet ceremonial man,
That when thou meet'st one, with enquiring eyes
Dost search, and like a needy broker prize

The silk and gold he wears, and to that rate
So high or low, dost raise thy formal hat:
That wilt consort none, until thou have known
What lands he hath in hope, or of his own,
As though all thy companions should make thee
Jointures, and marry thy dear company.
Why shouldst thou—that dost not only approve,
But in rank itchy lust, desire, and love
The nakedness and barrenness to enjoy,
Of thy plump muddy whore, or prostitute boy—
Hate virtue, though she be naked, and bare?
At birth, and death, our bodies naked are;
And till our souls be unapparrelled
Of bodies, they from bliss are banished.
Man's first blest state was naked, when by sin
He lost that, yet he was cloth'd but in beast's skin,
And in this course attire, which I now wear,
With God, and with the Muses I confer.
But since thou like a contrite penitent,
Charitably warn'd of thy sins, dost repent
These vanities, and giddinesses, lo
I shut my chamber door, and come, let's go.
But sooner may a cheap whore, who hath been
Worn by as many several men in sin,
As are black feathers, or musk-colour hose,
Name her child's right true father, 'mongst all those:
Sooner may one guess, who shall bear away
The Infanta of London, heir to an India;
And sooner may a gulling weather spy
By drawing forth heaven's scheme tell certainly
What fashioned hats, or ruffs, or suits next year
Our subtle-witted antic youths will wear;

Than thou, when thou depart'st from me, canst show
Whither, why, when, or with whom thou wouldst go.
But how shall I be pardon'd my offence
That thus have sinn'd against my conscience?
Now we are in the street; he first of all
Improvidently proud, creeps to the wall,
And so imprisoned, and hemmed in by me
Sells for a little state his liberty;
Yet though he cannot skip forth now to greet
Every fine silken painted fool we meet,
He them to him with amorous smiles allures,
And grins, smacks, shrugs, and such an itch endures,
As 'prentices, or school-boys which do know
Of some gay sport abroad, yet dare not go.
And as fiddlers stop lowest, at highest sound,
So to the most brave, stoops he nigh'st the ground.
But to a grave man, he doth move no more
Than the wise politic horse would heretofore,
Or thou O elephant or ape wilt do,
When any names the King of Spain to you.
Now leaps he upright, jogs me, and cries, 'Do you see
Yonder well-favoured youth?' 'Which?' 'Oh, 'tis he
That dances so divinely'; 'O,' said I,
'Stand still, must you dance here for company?'
He drooped, we went, till one—which did excel
Th'Indians, in drinking his tobacco well—
Met us; they talk'd; I whispered, 'Let us go,
'T may be you smell him not, truly I do';
He hears not me, but, on the other side
A many-coloured peacock having spied,
Leaves him and me; I for my lost sheep stay;
He follows, overtakes, goes on the way,

Saying, 'Him whom I last left, all repute
For his device, in handsoming a suit,
To judge of lace, pink, panes, print, cut, and pleat
Of all the court, to have the best conceit';
'Our dull comedians want him, let him go;
But O, God strengthen thee, why stoop'st thou so?'
'Why? he hath travelled'; 'Long?' 'No; but to me
(Which understand none) he doth seem to be
Perfect French, and Italian'; I replied,
'So is the pox'; he answered not, but spied
More men of sort, of parts, and qualities;
At last his Love he in a window spies,
And like light dew exhal'd, he flings from me
Violently ravish'd to his lechery.
Many were there, he could command no more;
He quarrell'd, fought, bled, and turn'd out of door
Directly came to me hanging the head,
And constantly a while must keep his bed.

SATIRE II

Sir; though—I thank God for it—I do hate
Perfectly all this town, yet there's one state
In all ill things so excellently best,
That hate, towards them, breeds pity towards the rest.
Though poetry indeed be such a sin
As I think that brings dearths, and Spaniards in,
Though like the pestilence and old fashion'd love,
Riddlingly it catch men; and doth remove
Never, till it be starv'd out; yet their state
Is poor, disarm'd, like papists, not worth hate.
One (like a wretch, which at Bar judg'd as dead,
Yet prompts him which stands next, and cannot read,
And saves his life) gives idiot actors means
—Starving himself—to live by his labor'd scenes;
As in some organ, puppets dance above
And bellows pant below, which them do move.
One would move love by rhymes; but witchcraft's charms
Bring not now their old fears, nor their old harms:
Rams, and slings now are silly battery,
Pistolets are the best artillery.
And they who write to lords, rewards to get,
Are they not like singers at doors for meat?
And they who write, because all write, have still
That excuse for writing, and for writing ill.
But he is worst, who—beggarly—doth chaw
Others' wits' fruits, and in his ravenous maw
Rankly digested, doth those things out-spew,
As his own things; and they are his own, 'tis true,
For if one eat my meat, though it be known
The meat was mine, th'excrement is his own.

But these do me no harm, nor they which use
To outdo Dildoes, and out-usure Jews;
To out-drink the sea, to out-swear the Litany;
Who with sins all kinds as familiar be
As confessors; and for whose sinful sake
Schoolmen new tenements in hell must make:
Whose strange sins, canonists could hardly tell
In which commandement's large receipt they dwell.
But these punish themselves; the insolence
Of Coscus only breeds my just offence,
Whom time—which rots all, and makes botches pox,
And plodding on, must make a calf an ox—
Hath made a lawyer, which was—alas—of late
But scarce a poet; jollier of this state,
Than are new benefic'd ministers, he throws
Like nets or lime-twigs, whereso'er he goes,
His title of barrister, on every wench,
And woos in language of the pleas, and bench:
'A motion, Lady'; 'Speak Coscus'; 'I have been
In love, ever since tricesimo of the Queen,
Continual claims I have made, injunctions got
To stay my rival's suit, that he should not
Proceed.' 'Spare mee'; 'In Hilary term I went,
You said, if I returned next 'size in Lent,
I should be in remitter of your grace;
In th'interim my letters should take place
Of affidavits': words, words, which would tear
The tender labyrinth of a soft maid's ear,
More, more, then ten Sclavonians scolding, more
Than when winds in our ruin'd abbeys roar.
When sick with poetry, and possessed with Muse
Thou wast, and mad, I hop'd; but men which choose

Law practice for mere gain, bold soul, repute
Worse than imbrothel'd strumpets prostitute.
Now like an owl-like watchman, he must walk
His hand still at a bill, now he must talk
Idly, like prisoners, which whole months will swear
That only suretyship hath brought them there,
And to every suitor lie in everything,
Like a king's favourite, yea like a king;
Like a wedge in a block, wring to the bar,
Bearing like asses, and more shameless far
Then carted whores, lie, to the grave judge; for
Bastardy abounds not in kings' titles, nor
Simony and sodomy in churchmen's lives,
As these things do in him; by these he thrives.
Shortly—as the sea—he will compass all our land;
From Scots, to Wight; from Mount, to Dover strand.
And spying heirs melting with luxury,
Satan will not joy at their sins, as he.
For as a thrifty wench scrapes kitchen stuff,
And barrelling the droppings, and the snuff,
Of wasting candles, which in thirty year
—Relic-like kept—perchance buys wedding gear;
Piecemeal he gets lands, and spends as much time
Wringing each acre, as men pulling prime.
In parchments then, large as his fields, he draws
Assurances, big, as gloss'd civil laws,
So huge, that men—in our time's forwardness—
Are Fathers of the Church for writing less.
These he writes not; nor for these written pays,
Therefore spares no length; as in those first days
When Luther was professed, he did desire
Short *Pater nosters*, saying as a friar

Each day his beads, but having left those laws,
Adds to Christ's prayer, the power and glory clause.
But when he sells or changes land, he impairs
His writings, and—unwatch'd—leaves out, *ses heires*,
As slyly as any commenter goes by
Hard words, or sense; or in Divinity
As controverters, in vouch'd texts, leave out
Shrewd words, which might against them clear the
  doubt.
Where are those spread woods which cloth'd heretofore
Those bought lands? not built, not burnt within door.
Where's th'old landlord's troops, and alms? In great halls
Carthusian fasts, and fulsome bacchanals
Equally I hate; means bless; in rich men's homes
I bid kill some beasts, but no hecatombs,
None starve, none surfeit so; but O we allow
Good works as good, but out of fashion now,
Like old rich wardrobes; but my words none draws
Within the vast reach of the huge statute laws.

SATIRE III

Kind pity chokes my spleen; brave scorn forbids
Those tears to issue which swell my eyelids;
I must not laugh, nor weep sins and be wise;
Can railing, then, cure these worn maladies?
Is not our mistress, fair Religion,
As worthy of all our souls' devotion
As virtue was in the first blinded age?
Are not heaven's joys as valiant to assuage
Lusts, as earth's honour was to them? Alas,
As we do them in means, shall they surpass
Us in the end? and shall thy father's spirit
Meet blind philosophers in heaven, whose merit
Of strict life may be imputed faith, and hear
Thee, whom he taught so easy ways and near
To follow, damn'd? O, if thou dar'st, fear this;
This fear great courage and high valour is.
Dar'st thou aid mutinous Dutch, and dar'st thou lay
Thee in ships' wooden sepulchres, a prey
To leaders' rage, to storms, to shot, to dearth?
Dar'st thou dive seas, and dungeons of the earth?
Hast thou courageous fire to thaw the ice
Of frozen North discoveries? and thrice
Colder than salamanders, like divine
Children in th' oven, fires of Spain, and the line,
Whose countries limbecs to our bodies be,
Canst thou for gain bear? and must every he
Which cries not, 'Goddess', to thy mistress, draw
Or eat thy poisonous words? Courage of straw!
O desperate coward, wilt thou seem bold, and
To thy foes and his, who made thee to stand

Sentinel in his world's garrison, thus yield,
And for forbidden wars leave th' appointed field?
Know thy foes: the foul devil, whom thou
Strivest to please, for hate, not love, would allow
Thee fain his whole realm to be quit; and as
The world's all parts wither away and pass,
So the world's self, thy other lov'd foe, is
In her decrepit wane, and thou loving this,
Dost love a wither'd and worn strumpet; last,
Flesh (itself's death) and joys which flesh can taste,
Thou lovest, and thy fair goodly soul, which doth
Give this flesh power to taste joy, thou dost loathe.
Seek true religion. O where? Mirreus,
Thinking her unhous'd here, and fled from us,
Seeks her at Rome; there, because he doth know
That she was there a thousand years ago,
He loves her rags so, as we here obey
The statecloth where the prince sate yesterday.
Crantz to such brave loves will not be enthrall'd,
But loves her only, who at Geneva is call'd
Religion, plain, simple, sullen, young,
Contemptuous, yet unhandsome; as among
Lecherous humours, there is one that judges
No wenches wholesome, but coarse country drudges.
Graius stays still at home here, and because
Some preachers, vile ambitious bawds, and laws,
Still new like fashions, bid him think that she
Which dwells with us is only perfect, he
Embraceth her whom his godfathers will
Tender to him, being tender, as wards still
Take such wives as their guardians offer, or
Pay values. Careless Phrygius doth abhor

All, because all cannot be good, as one
Knowing some women whores, dares marry none.
Graccus loves all as one, and thinks that so
As women do in divers countries go
In divers habits, yet are still one kind,
So doth, so is Religion; and this blind-
ness too much light breeds; but unmoved, thou
Of force must one, and forc'd, but one allow,
And the right; ask thy father which is she,
Let him ask his; though truth and falsehood be
Near twins, yet truth a little elder is;
Be busy to seek her; believe me this,
He's not of none, nor worst, that seeks the best.
To adore, or scorn an image, or protest,
May all be bad; doubt wisely; in strange way
To stand inquiring right, is not to stray;
To sleep, or run wrong, is. On a huge hill,
Cragged and steep, Truth stands, and he that will
Reach her, about must and about must go,
And what the hill's suddenness resists, win so.
Yet strive so that before age, death's twilight,
Thy soul rest, for none can work in that night.
To will implies delay, therefore now do;
Hard deeds, the body's pains; hard knowledge too
The mind's endeavours reach, and mysteries
Are like the sun, dazzling, yet plain to all eyes.
Keep the truth which thou hast found; men do not stand
In so ill case, that God hath with his hand
Sign'd kings' blank charters to kill whom they hate;
Nor are they vicars, but hangmen to fate.
Fool and wretch, wilt thou let thy soul be tied
To man's laws, by which she shall not be tried

At the last day? Or will it then boot thee
To say a Philip, or a Gregory,
A Harry, or a Martin, taught thee this?
Is not this excuse for mere contraries
Equally strong? Cannot both sides say so?
That thou mayest rightly obey power, her bounds know;
Those past, her nature and name is chang'd; to be
Then humble to her is idolatry.
As streams are, power is; those blessed flowers that dwell
At the rough stream's calm head, thrive and do well,
But having left their roots, and themselves given
To the stream's tyrannous rage, alas, are driven
Through mills, and rocks, and woods, and at last, almost
Consum'd in going, in the sea are lost.
So perish souls, which more choose men's unjust
Power from God claim'd, than God himself to trust.

SATIRE IV

Well; I may now receive, and die; my sin
Indeed is great, but I have been in
A purgatory, such as fear'd hell is
A recreation and scant map of this.
My mind, neither with pride's itch, nor yet
    hath been
Poison'd with love to see, or to be seen.
I had no suit there, nor new suit to show,
Yet went to court; but as Glaze which did go
To'a mass in jest, catch'd, was fain to disburse
The hundred marks, which is the statute's curse,
Before he 'scaped, so it pleas'd my destiny
—Guilty of my sin of going—to think me
As prone to all ill, and of good as forget-
ful, as proud, as lustful, and as much in debt,
As vain, as witless, and as false as they
Which dwell at court, for once going that way.
Therefore I suffer'd this; towards me did run
A thing more strange, than on Nile's slime the sun
E'r bred; or all which into Noah's Ark came;
A thing which would have pos'd Adam to name;
Stranger than seven antiquaries' studies,
Than Afric's monsters, Guiana's rarities;
Stranger than strangers; one, who for a Dane,
In the Danes' massacre had sure been slain,
If he had liv'd then; and without help dies,
When next the 'prentices 'gainst strangers rise.
One, whom the watch at noon lets scarce go by,
One, to whom the examining justice sure would cry,
'Sir, by your priesthood tell me what you are.'

His clothes were strange, though coarse; and black,
    though bare;
Sleeveless his jerkin was, and it had been
Velvet, but 'twas now—so much ground was seen—
Become tufftaffaty; and our children shall
See it plain rash awhile, then nought at all.
This thing hath travell'd, and, saith, speaks all tongues,
And only knoweth what to all states belongs,
Made of th'accents, and best phrase of all these,
He speaks one language; if strange meats displease,
Art can deceive, or hunger force my taste,
But pedant's motley tongue, soldier's bombast,
Mountebank's drug-tongue, nor the terms of law
Are strong enough preparatives, to draw
Me to bear this: yet I must be content
With his tongue, in his tongue, call'd compliment:
In which he can win widows, and pay scores,
Make men speak treason, cozen subtlest whores,
Out-flatter favourites, or outlie either
Jovius, or Surius, or both together.
He names me, and comes to me; I whisper, 'God!
How have I sinn'd, that thy wrath's furious rod,
This fellow, chooseth me?' He sayeth, 'Sir,
I love your judgement; whom do you prefer,
For the best linguist?' And I sillily
Said, that I thought Calepine's Dictionary;
'Nay, but of men, most sweet Sir'. Beza then,
Some Jesuits, and two reverend men
Of our two Academies, I named. There
He stopp'd me, and said, 'Nay, your apostles were
Good pretty linguists, and so Panurge was;
Yet a poor gentleman, all these may pass

By travail.' Then, as if he would have sold
His tongue, he prais'd it, and such wonders told
That I was fain to say, 'If you had liv'd, Sir,
Time enough to have been interpreter
To Babel's bricklayers, sure the Tower had stood.'
He adds, 'If of court life you knew the good,
You would leave loneness.' I said, 'Not alone
My loneness is. But Spartan's fashion,
To teach by painting drunkards, doth not last
Now; Aretine's pictures have made few chaste;
No more can princes' courts, though there be few
Better pictures of vice, teach me virtue.'
He, like to a high stretched lute string squeaked,
　　'O Sir,
'Tis sweet to talke of kings.' 'At Westminster,'
Said I, 'The man that keeps the Abbey tombs,
And for his price doth with whoever comes,
Of all our Harrys, and our Edwards talk,
From king to king and all their kin can walk:
Your ears shall hear nought, but kings; your eyes meet
Kings only; the way to it, is King Street.'
He smack'd, and cried, 'He's base, mechanic, coarse,
So are all your Englishmen in their discourse.
Are not your Frenchmen neat?' 'Mine? as you see,
I have but one Frenchman, look, he follows me.'
'Certes they are neatly cloth'd; I of this mind am,
Your only wearing is your grogaram.'
'Not so Sir, I have more.' Under this pitch
He would not fly; I chaff'd him; but as itch
Scratch'd into smart, and as blunt iron ground
Into an edge, hurts worse: so, I—fool—found,
Crossing hurt me; to fit my sullenness,

He to another key his style doth dress,
And asks, 'What news?' I tell him of new plays.
He takes my hand, and as a still, which stays
A semibrieve, 'twixt each drop, he niggardly,
As loath to enrich me, so tells many a lie.
More than ten Holinsheds, or Halls, or Stows,
Of trivial household trash he knows; he knows
When the Queen frown'd, or smil'd, and he knows what
A subtle statesman may gather of that;
He knows who loves; whom; and who by poison
Hastes to an office's reversion;
He knows who hath sold his land, and now doth beg
A licence, old iron, boots, shoes, and egg-
shells to transport; shortly boys shall not play
At span-counter, or blow-point, but they pay
Toll to some courtier; and wiser than all us,
He knows what lady is not painted; thus
He with home-meats tries me; I belch, spew, spit,
Look pale, and sickly, like a patient; yet
He thrusts on more; and as if he undertook
To say Gallo-Belgicus without book
Speaks of all states, and deeds, that have been since
The Spaniards came, to the loss of Amiens.
Like a big wife, at sight of loathed meat,
Ready to travail: so I sigh, and sweat
To hear this Macaron talk. In vain; for yet,
Either my humour, or his own to fit,
He like a privileged spy, whom nothing can
Discredit, libels now 'gainst each great man.
He names a price for every office paid;
He saith, our wars thrive ill, because delayed;
That offices are entail'd, and that there are

Perpetuities of them, lasting as far
As the last day; and that great officers,
Do with the pirates share, and Dunkirkers.
Who wastes in meat, in clothes, in horse, he notes;
Who loves whores, who boys, and who goats.
I more amazed than Circe's prisoners, when
They felt themselves turn beasts, felt my self then
Becoming traitor, and methought I saw
One of our giant Statutes ope his jaw
To suck me in; for hearing him, I found
That as burnt venom'd lechers do grow sound
By giving others their sores, I might grow
Guilty, and he free: therefore I did show
All signs of loathing; but since I am in,
I must pay mine, and my forefathers' sin
To the last farthing; therefore to my power
Toughly and stubbornly I bear this cross; but the hour
Of mercy now was come; he tries to bring
Me to pay a fine to 'scape his torturing,
And says, 'Sir, can you spare me?'; I said, 'Willingly'.
'Nay, Sir, can you spare me a crown?' Thankfully I
Gave it, as ransom; but as fiddlers, still,
Though they be paid to be gone, yet needs will
Thrust one more jig upon you: so did he
With his long complimental thanks vex me.
But he is gone, thanks to his needy want,
And the prerogative of my crown: scant
His thanks were ended, when I—which did see
All the court fill'd with more strange things than he—
Ran from thence with such or more haste than one
Who fears more actions doth make from prison.
At home in wholesome solitariness

My precious soul began, the wretchedness
Of suitors at court to mourn, and a trance
Like his, who dreamed he saw hell, did advance
Itself on me; such men as he saw there
I saw at court, and worse, and more; low fear
Becomes the guilty, not the accuser; then,
Shall I, none's slave, of high born or rais'd men
Fear frowns? And, my mistresse Truth, betray thee
To th'huffing braggart, puffed nobility?
No, no, thou which since yesterday hast been
Almost about the whole world, hast thou seen,
O Sun, in all thy journey, vanity
Such as swells the bladder of our court? I
Think he which made your waxen garden, and
Transported it from Italy to stand
With us, at London, flouts our presence, for
Just such gay painted things, which no sap, nor
Taste have in them, ours are; and natural
Some of the stocks are, their fruits, bastard all.
'Tis ten a-clock and past; all whom the Mues,
Baloune, Tennis, Dyet, or the stews,
Had all the morning held, now the second
Time made ready, that day, in flocks, are found
In the presence, and I—God pardon me—
As fresh, and sweet their apparels be, as be
The fields they sold to buy them; 'For a King
Those hose are', cry the flatterers; and bring
Them next week to the theatre to sell;
Wants reach all states; me seems they do as well
At stage, as court; all are players; whoe'r looks
—For themselves dare not go—o'er Cheapside books,
Shall find their wardrobe's inventory. Now,

The ladies come; as pirates, which do know
That there came weak ships fraught with cochineal,
The men board them; and praise, as they think, well,
Their beauties; they the men's wits; both are bought.
Why good wits ne'er wear scarlet gowns, I thought
This cause: these men, men's wits for speeches buy,
And women buy all reds which scarlets dye.
He call'd her beauty lime-twigs, her hair net;
She fears her drugs ill laid, her hair loose set.
Would not Heraclitus laugh to see Macrine,
From hat, to shoe, himself at door refine,
As if the presence were a moschite, and lift
His skirts and hose, and call his clothes to shrift,
Making them confess not only mortal
Great stains and holes in them; but venial
Feathers and dust, wherewith they fornicate;
And then by Dürer's rules survey the state
Of his each limb, and with strings the odds tries
Of his neck to his leg, and waist to thighs.
So in immaculate clothes, and symmetry
Perfect as circles, with such nicety
As a young preacher at his first time goes
To preach, he enters, and a lady which owes
Him not so much as good will, he arrests,
And unto her protests protests protests
So much as at Rome would serve to have thrown
Ten cardinals into the Inquisition;
And whisperd 'by Jesu', so often, that a
Pursuivant would have ravish'd him away
For saying of our Lady's psalter; but 'tis fit
That they each other plague, they merit it.
But here comes Glorius that will plague them both,

Who, in the other extreme, only doth
Call a rough carelessness, good fashion;
Whose cloak his spurs tear; whom he spits on
He cares not; his ill words do no harm
To him; he rusheth in, as if 'Arme, arme',
He meant to cry; and though his face be as ill
As theirs which in old hangings whip Christ, yet still
He strives to look worse, he keeps all in awe;
Jests like a licenc'd fool, commands like law.
Tired, now I leave this place, and but pleased so
As men which from gaols to execution go,
Go through the great chamber—why is it hung
With the seven deadly sins?. Being among
Those Ascaparts, men big enough to throw
Charing Cross for a bar, men that do know
No token of worth, but Queen's man, and fine
Living, barrels of beef, flagons of wine;
I shook like a spied spy. Preachers which are
Seas of wit and arts, you can, then dare,
Drown the sins of this place, for, for me
Which am but a scarce brook, it enough shall be
To wash the stains away; though I yet
With Machabee's modesty, the known merit
Of my work lessen: yet some wise man shall,
I hope, esteem my writs canonical.

SATIRE V

Thou shalt not laugh in this leaf, Muse, nor they
Whom any pity warms; he which did lay
Rules to make courtiers, (he being understood
May make good courtiers, but who courtiers good?)
Frees from the sting of jests all who in extreme
Are wretched or wicked: of these two a theme
Charity and liberty give me. What is he
Who officers' rage, and suitors' misery
Can write, and jest? If all things be in all,
As I think, since all, which were, are, and shall
Be, be made of the same elements:
Each thing, each thing implies or represents.
Then man is a world; in which, officers
Are the vast ravishing seas; and suitors,
Springs; now full, now shallow, now dry; which, to
That which drowns them, run. These self reasons do
Prove the world a man, in which officers
Are the devouring stomach, and suitors
Th'excrements, which they void. All men are dust;
How much worse are suitors, who to men's lust
Are made preys? O worse than dust, or worms' meat,
For they do eat you now, whose selves worms shall eat.
They are the mills which grind you, yet you are
The wind which drives them; and a wastful war
Is fought against you, and you fight it; they
Adulterate law, and you prepare their way
Like wittals; th'issue your own ruin is.
Greatest and fairest Empress, know you this?
Alas, no more than Thames' calm head doth know
Whose meads her arms drown, or whose corn o'erflow:

You Sir, whose righteousness she loves, whom I
By having leave to serve, am most richly
For service paid, authoriz'd, now begin
To know and weed out this enormous sin.
O Age of rusty iron! Some better wit
Call it some worse name, if aught equal it;
The Iron Age that was, when justice was sold; now
Injustice is sold dearer far. Allow
All demands, fees, and duties; gamsters, anon
The money which you sweat, and swear for, is gone
Into other hands: so controverted lands
'Scape, like Angelica, the strivers' hands.
If law be in the judge's heart, and he
Have no heart to resist letter, or fee,
Where wilt thou appeal? Power of the courts below
Flow from the first main head, and these can throw
Thee, if they suck thee in, to misery,
To fetters, halters; but if the injury
Steel thee to dare complain, alas, thou go'st
Against the stream, when upwards: when thou art most
Heavy and most faint; and in these labours they,
'Gainst whom thou shouldst complain, will in the way
Become great seas, o'er which, when thou shalt be
Forced to make golden bridges, thou shalt see
That all thy gold was drown'd in them before;
All things follow their like, only who have may have
     more.
Judges are gods; he who made and said them so,
Meant not that men should be forc'd to them to go,
By means of angels; when supplications
We send to God, to Dominations,
Powers, Cherubins, and all heaven's courts, if we

Should pay fees as here, daily bread would be
Scarce to kings; so 'tis. Would it not anger
A stoic, a coward, yea a martyr,
To see a pursuivant come in, and call
All his clothes, copes; books, primers; and all
His plate, chalices; and mistake them away,
And ask a fee for coming? O, ne'er may
Fair Law's white reverend name be strumpeted,
To warrant thefts: she is established
Recorder to Destiny, on earth, and she
Speaks Fate's words, and but tells us who must be
Rich, who poor, who in chairs, who in gaols:
She is all fair, but yet hath foul long nails,
With which she scratcheth suitors; in bodies
Of men, so in law, nails are th'extremities,
So officers stretch to more than Law can do,
As our nails reach what no else part comes to.
Why barest thou to yon officer? Fool, hath he
Got those goods, for which erst men bared to thee?
Fool, twice, thrice, thou hast bought wrong, and now
    hungerly
Beg'st right; but that dole comes not till these die.
Thou hadst much, and law's Urim and Thummim try
Thou wouldst for more; and for all hast paper
Enough to clothe all the Great Carrack's pepper,
Sell that, and by that thou much more shalt leese,
Than Haman, when he sold his antiquities.

SECTION V:
VERSE LETTERS

The Storm

To Mr Christopher Brooke (from the Island Voyage with the Earl of Essex)

Thou which art I, ('tis nothing to be so)
Thou which art still thyself, by these shalt know
Part of our passage; and, a hand, or eye
By Hilliard drawn, is worth a history,
By a worse painter made; and—without pride—
When by thy judgement they are dignifi'd,
My lines are such. 'Tis the pre-eminence
Of friendship only to impute excellence.
England, to whom we owe, what we be, and have,
Sad that her sons did seek a foreign grave
—For, Fate's, or Fortune's drifts none can soothsay,
Honour and misery have one face, and way—
From out her pregnant entrails sigh'd a wind,
Which at th'air's middle marble room did find
Such strong resistance, that itself it threw
Downward again; and so when it did view
How in the port, our fleet dear time did leese,
Withering like prisoners, which lie but for fees,
Mildly it kissed our sails, and, fresh and sweet
As, to a stomach starv'd, whose insides meet,
Meat comes, it came; and swole our sails, when we
So joyed, as Sara her swelling joy'd to see.
But 'twas but so kind, as our countrymen,
Which bring friends one day's way, and leave them then.
Then like two mighty kings, which dwelling far
Asunder, meet against a third to war,
The South and West winds joined, and, as they blew,
Waves like a rolling trench before them threw.

Sooner than you read this line, did the gale,
Like shot, not fear'd till felt, our sails assail;
And what at first was call'd a gust, the same
Hath now a storm's, anon, a tempest's name.
Jonas, I pity thee, and curse those men
Who, when the storm raged most, did wake thee then.
Sleep is pain's easiest salve, and doth fulfil
All offices of death, except to kill.
But when I waked, I saw that I saw not.
I, and the sun, which should teach me, had forgot
East, west, day, night, and I could only say,
If the world had lasted, now it had been day.
Thousands our noises were, yet we 'mongst all
Could none by his right name, but thunder, call:
Lightning was all our light, and it rain'd more
Than if the sun had drunk the sea before;
Some coffin'd in their cabins lie, equally
Griev'd that they are not dead, and yet must die.
And as sin-burd'ned souls from graves will creep,
At the last day, some forth their cabins peep:
And tremblingly ask what news, and do hear so,
Like jealous husbands, what they would not know.
Some sitting on the hatches, would seem there,
With hideous gazing to fear away fear.
Then note they the ship's sicknesses, the mast
Shak'd with an ague, and the hold and waist
With a salt dropsy clogg'd, and all our tacklings
Snapping, like too-high-stretched treble strings.
And from our totterd sailes, rags drop down so,
As from one hang'd in chains a year ago.
Even our ordnance plac'd for our defence,
Strive to break loose, and 'scape away from thence.

Pumping hath tired our men, and what's the gain?
Seas into seas thrown, we suck in again;
Hearing hath deaf'd our sailors: and if they
Knew how to hear, there's none knows what to say.
Compar'd to these storms, death is but a qualm,
Hell somewhat lightsome, and the Bermuda calm.
Darkness, light's elder brother, his birth-right
Claims o'er this world, and to heaven hath chas'd light.
All things are one, and that one none can be,
Since all forms uniform deformity
Doth cover, so that wee, except God say
Another Fiat, shall have no more day.
So violent yet long these furies be,
That though thine absence starve me, I wish not thee.

The Calm

Our storm is past, and that storm's tyrannous rage
A stupid calm, but nothing it, doth 'suage.
The fable is inverted, and far more
A block afflicts, now, than a stork before.
Storms chafe, and soon wear out themselves, or us;
In calms, heaven laughs to see us languish thus.
As steady as I can wish that my thoughts were,
Smooth as thy mistress' glass, or what shines there,
The sea is now; and, as the isles which we
Seek, when we can move, our ships rooted be.
As water did in storms, now pitch runs out;
As lead, when a fired church becomes one spout.
And all our beauty and our trim decays,
Like courts removing, or like ended plays.
The fighting-place now seamen's rags supply;
And all the tackling is a frippery.
No use of lanthorns; and in one place lay
Feathers and dust, today and yesterday.
Earth's hollownesses, which the world's lungs are,
Have no more wind than the upper vault of air.
We can nor lost friends nor sought foes recover,
But meteor-like, save that we move not, hover.
Only the calenture together draws
Dear friends, which meet dead in great fishes' jaws;
And on the hatches, as on altars, lies
Each one, his own priest and own sacrifice.
Who live, that miracle do multiply,
Where walkers in hot ovens do not die.
If in despite of these we swim, that hath
No more refreshing than our brimstone bath;

But from the sea into the ship we turn,
Like parboil'd wretches, on the coals to burn.
Like Bajazet encaged, the shepherds' scoff,
Or like slack-sinew'd Samson, his hair off,
Languish our ships. Now as a myriad
Of ants durst th' emperor's loved snake invade,
The crawling gallies, sea-gaols, finny chips,
Might brave our pinnaces, now bed-rid ships.
Whether a rotten state, and hope of gain,
Or to disuse me from the queasy pain
Of being beloved and loving, or the thirst
Of honour or fair death, out-push'd me first,
I lose my end; for here, as well as I,
A desperate may live, and coward die.
Stag, dog, and all which from or towards flies,
Is paid with life or prey, or doing dies.
Fate grudges us all, and doth subtly lay
A scourge, 'gainst which we all forget to pray.
He that at sea prays for more wind, as well
Under the poles may beg cold, heat in hell.
What are we then? How little more, alas,
Is man now, than before he was? He was
Nothing; for us, we are for nothing fit;
Chance, or ourselves, still disproportion it.
We have no power, no will, no sense; I lie,
I should not then thus feel this misery.

SECTION VI:
DIVINE POEMS

The Cross

Since Christ embraced the Cross itself, dare I
His image, th' image of his Cross deny?
Would I have profit by the sacrifice,
And dare the chosen altar to despise?
It bore all other sins, but is it fit
That it should bear the sin of scorning it?
Who from the picture would avert his eye,
How would he fly his pains, who there did die?
From me, no pulpit, nor misgrounded law,
Nor scandal taken, shall this Cross withdraw,
It shall not, for it cannot; for, the loss
Of this Cross, were to me another cross;
Better were worse, for, no affliction,
No cross is so extreme, as to have none.
Who can blot out the Cross, which th' instrument
Of God, dewed on me in the Sacrament?
Who can deny me power, and liberty
To stretch mine arms, and mine own cross to be?
Swim, and at every stroke, thou art thy cross,
The mast and yard make one, where seas do toss.
Look down, thou spiest out crosses in small things;
Look up, thous seest birds raised on crossed wings;
All the globe's frame, and sphere's, is nothing else
But the meridians crossing parallels.
Material crosses then, good physic be,
And yet spiritual have chief dignity.
These for extracted chemic medicine serve,
And cure much better, and as well preserve;

Then are you your own physic, or need none,
When stilled, or purged by tribulation.
For when that Cross ungrudged unto you sticks,
Then are you to yourself a crucifix.
As perchance, carvers do not faces make,
But that away, which hid them there, do take:
Let crosses, so, take what hid Christ in thee,
And be his image, or not his, but he.
But, as oft alchemists do coiners prove,
So may a self-despising, get self-love.
And then as worst surfeits of best eats be,
So is pride issued from humility.
For, 'tis no child, but monster; therefore cross
Your joy in crosses, else, 'tis double loss,
And cross thy sense, else, both they, and thou
Must perish soon, and to destruction bow.
For if the'eye seek good objects, and will take
No cross from bad, we cannot 'scape a snake.
So with harsh, hard, sour, stinking, cross the rest,
Make them indifferent; call nothing best.
But most the eye needs crossing, that can roam,
And move; to th' others th' objects must come home.
And cross thy heart: for that in man alone
Points downwards, and hath palpitation.
Cross those dejection, when it downward tends,
And when it to forbidden heights pretends.
And as the brain through bony walls doth vent
By sutures, which a cross's form present,
So when thy brain works, ere thou utter it,
Cross and correct concupiscence of wit.

Be covetous of crosses, let none fall.
Cross no man else, but cross thyself in all.
Then doth the Cross of Christ work fruitfully
Within our hearts, when we love harmlessly
That Cross's pictures much, and with more care
That Cross's children, which our crosses are.

Good Friday, 1613. Riding Westward

Let man's soul be a sphere, and then, in this,
The intelligence that moves, devotion is;
And as the other spheres, by being grown
Subject to foreign motion, lose their own,
And being by others hurried every day,
Scarce in a year their natural form obey;
Pleasure or business, so, our souls admit
For their first mover, and are whirl'd by it.
Hence is't, that I am carried towards the west,
This day, when my soul's form bends to the east.
There I should see a sun, by rising set,
And by that setting endless day beget.
But that Christ on this Cross did rise and fall,
Sin had eternally benighted all.
Yet dare I' almost be glad, I do not see
That spectacle of too much weight for me.
Who sees God's face, that is self-life, must die;
What a death were it then to see God die?
It made his own lieutenant, Nature, shrink,
It made his footstool crack, and the sun wink.
Could I behold those hands, which span the poles
And tune all spheres at once, pierced with those holes?
Could I behold that endless height, which is
Zenith to us, and our antipodes,
Humbled below us? Or that blood, which is
The seat of all our souls, if not of his,
Made dirt of dust, or that flesh which was worn
By God for his apparel, ragg'd and torn?
If on these things I durst not look, durst I
Upon his miserable mother cast mine eye,

Who was God's partner here, and furnish'd thus
Half of that sacrifice which ransom'd us?
Though these things as I ride be from mine eye,
They're present yet unto my memory,
For that looks towards them; and thou look'st towards me,
O Saviour, as thou hang'st upon the tree.
I turn my back to thee, but to receive
Corrections till thy mercies bid thee leave.
O think me worth thine anger, punish me,
Burn off my rust, and my deformity;
Restore thine image, so much, by thy grace,
That thou mayst know me, and I'll turn my face.

A Hymn to God the Father

Wilt thou forgive that sin where I begun,
    Which is my sin, though it were done before?
Wilt thou forgive that sin through which I run,
    And do run still, though still I do deplore?
      When thou hast done, thou hast not done,
        For I have more.

Wilt thou forgive that sin by which I have won
    Others to sin, and made my sin their door?
Wilt thou forgive that sin which I did shun
    A year or two, but wallowed in a score?
      When thou hast done, thou hast not done,
        For I have more.

I have a sin of fear, that when I have spun
    My last thread, I shall perish on the shore;
But swear by thyself, that at my death thy Son
    Shall shine as he shines now and heretofore;
      And, having done that, thou hast done,
        I fear no more.

La Corona

1. *Deign at my hands this crown of prayer and praise,*
Weav'd in my low devout melancholy,
Thou which of good hast, yea, art treasury,
All changing unchang'd Ancient of days.
But do not, with a vile crown of fraile bays,
Reward my muse's white sincerity,
But what thy thorny crown gain'd, that give me,
A crown of glory, which doth flower always;
The ends crown our works, but thou crown'st our ends,
For at our end begins our endless rest.
The first last end, now zealously possessed,
With a strong sober thirst, my soul attends.
'Tis time that heart and voice be lifted high,
Salvation to all that will is nigh.

Annunciation
2. *Salvation to all that will is nigh;*
That all, which always is all everywhere,
Which cannot sin, and yet all sins must bear,
Which cannot die, yet cannot choose but die,
Lo, faithful Virgin, yields himself to lie
In prison, in thy womb; and though he there
Can take no sin, nor thou give, yet he will wear,
Taken from thence, flesh, which death's force may try.
Ere by the spheres time was created, thou
Wast in his mind, who is thy son, and brother;
Whom thou conceiv'st, conceiv'd; yea, thou art now
Thy Maker's maker, and thy Father's mother;
Thou hast light in dark; and shutt'st in little room,
Immensity, cloistered in thy dear womb.

Nativity

3. *Immensity, cloistered in thy dear womb,*
Now leaves his welbelov'd imprisonment,
There he hath made himself to his intent
Weak enough, now into our world to come;
But O, for thee, for him, hath th'inn no room?
Yet lay him in this stall, and from the orient,
Stars, and wise men will travel to prevent
Th'effect of Herod's jealous general doom.
See'st thou, my soul, with thy faith's eyes, how he
Which fills all place, yet none holds him, doth lie?
Was not his pity towards thee wondrous high,
That would have need to be pitied by thee?
Kiss him, and with him into Egypt go,
With his kind mother, who partakes thy woe.

Temple

4. *With his kind mother, who partakes thy woe,*
Joseph turn back; see where your child doth sit,
Blowing, yea blowing out those sparks of wit,
Which himself on the doctors did bestow;
The Word but lately could not speake, and lo,
It suddenly speaks wonders; whence comes it,
That all which was, and all which should be writ,
A shallow seeming child should deeply know?
His Godhead was not soul to his manhood,
Nor had time mellowed him to this ripeness,
But as for one which hath a long taske, 'tis good,
With the Sun to begin his business,
He in his age's morning thus began
By miracles exceeding power of man.

Crucifying

5. By miracles exceeding power of man,
He faith in some, envy in some begat,
For, what weak spirits admire, ambitious hate;
In both affections many to him ran,
But O! the worst are most, they will and can,
Alas, and do, unto the immaculate,
Whose creature Fate is, now prescribe a fate,
Measuring self-life's infinity to a span,
Nay to an inch. Lo, where condemned he
Bears his own cross, with pain, yet by and by
When it bears him, he must bear more and die.
Now thou art lifted up, draw me to thee,
And at thy death giving such liberal dole,
Moist, with one drop of thy blood, my dry soul.

Resurrection

6. Moist, with one drop of thy blood, my dry soul
Shall (though she now be in extreme degree
Too stony hard, and yet too fleshly) be
Freed by that drop, from being starv'd, hard, or foul,
And life, by this death abled, shall control
Death, whom thy death slew; nor shall to me
Fear of first or last death, bring misery,
If in thy little book my name thou enrol,
Flesh in that long sleep is not putrified,
But made that there, of which, and for which 'twas;
Nor can by other means be glorified.
May then sin's sleep, and death's soon from me pass,
That waked from both, I again risen may
Salute the last and everlasting day.

Ascension

7. *Salute the last and everlasting day,*
Joy at the uprising of this sun, and son,
Ye whose just tears, or tribulation
Have purely washed, or burnt your drossy clay;
Behold the Highest, parting hence away,
Lightens the dark clouds, which he treads upon,
Nor doth he by ascending, show alone,
But first he, and he first enters the way.
O strong ram, which hast batter'd heaven for me,
Mild lamb, which with thy blood, hast mark'd the path;
Bright torch, which shin'st, that I the way may see,
O, with thy own blood quench thy own just wrath,
And if thy Holy Spirit, my Muse did raise,
Deign at my hands this crown of prayer and praise.

HOLY SONNETS

Thou hast made me, and shall thy work decay?
Repair me now, for now mine end doth haste;
I run to death, and death meets me as fast,
And all my pleasures are like yesterday.
I dare not move my dim eyes any way;
Despair behind, and Death before doth cast
Such terror, and my feeble flesh doth waste
By sin in it, which it towards hell doth weigh.
Only Thou art above, and when towards Thee
By Thy leave I can look, I rise again;
But our old subtle foe so tempteth me,
That not one hour myself I can sustain.
Thy grace may wing me to prevent his art
And Thou like adamant draw mine iron heart.

⁓

As due by many titles I resign
Myself to thee, O God, first I was made
By Thee, and for Thee, and when I was decay'd
Thy blood bought that, the which before was Thine.
I am Thy son, made with Thyself to shine,
Thy servant, whose pains Thou hast still repaid,
Thy sheep, Thine image, and—till I betray'd
Myself—a temple of Thy Spirit divine.
Why doth the devil then usurp on me?
Why doth he steal, nay ravish, that's Thy right?
Except Thou rise and for Thine own work fight.
O! I shall soon despair, when I shall see
That Thou lov'st mankind well, yet wilt not choose me,
And Satan hates me, yet is loth to lose me.

O! might those sighs and tears return again
Into my breast and eyes, which I have spent,
That I might in this holy discontent
Mourn with some fruit, as I have mourn'd in vain.
In mine idolatry what showers of rain
Mine eyes did waste, what griefs my heart did rent!
That sufferance was my sin, I now repent;
'Cause I did suffer, I must suffer pain.
Th' hydroptic drunkard, and night-scouting thief,
The itchy lecher, and self-tickling proud
Have the remembrance of past joys, for relief
Of coming ills. To poor me is allow'd
No ease; for long, yet vehement grief hath been
The effect and cause, the punishment and sin.

O, my black soul, now thou art summoned
By sickness, Death's herald and champion;
Thou 'rt like a pilgrim, which abroad hath done
Treason, and durst not turn to whence he's fled;
Or like a thief, which till death's doom be read,
Wisheth himself deliver'd from prison,
But damn'd and haled to execution,
Wisheth that still he might be imprisoned.
Yet grace, if thou repent, thou canst not lack;
But who shall give thee that grace to begin?
O, make thyself with holy mourning black,
And red with blushing, as thou art with sin;
Or wash thee in Christ's blood, which hath this might,
That being red, it dyes red souls to white.

I am a little world made cunningly
Of elements and an angelic sprite;
But black sin hath betray'd to endless night
My world's both parts, and, O, both parts must die.
You which beyond that heaven which was most high
Have found new spheres, and of new lands can write,
Pour new seas in mine eyes, that so I might
Drown my world with my weeping earnestly,
Or wash it if it must be drown'd no more.
But O, it must be burnt; alas! the fire
Of lust and envy have burnt it heretofore,
And made it fouler; let their flames retire,
And burn me, O Lord, with a fiery zeal
Of Thee and Thy house, which doth in eating heal.

This is my play's last scene; here heavens appoint
My pilgrimage's last mile; and my race
Idly, yet quickly run, hath this last pace;
My span's last inch, my minute's latest point;
And gluttonous Death will instantly unjoint
My body and soul, and I shall sleep a space;
But my ever-waking part shall see that face
Whose fear already shakes my every joint.
Then, as my soul to heaven her first seat, takes flight,
And earth-born body in the earth shall dwell,
So fall my sins, that all may have their right,
To where they're bred and would press me to hell.
Impute me righteous, thus purged of evil,
For thus I leave the world, the flesh, the devil.

At the round earth's imagined corners blow
Your trumpets, angels, and arise, arise
From death, you numberless infinities
Of souls, and to your scattered bodies go;
All whom the flood did, and fire shall o'erthrow,
All whom war, dearth, age, agues, tyrannies,
Despair, law, chance hath slain, and you, whose eyes
Shall behold God, and never taste death's woe.
But let them sleep, Lord, and me mourn a space;
For, if above all these my sins abound,
'Tis late to ask abundance of Thy grace
When we are there. Here on this lowly ground,
Teach me how to repent, for that's as good
As if Thou hadst seal'd my pardon with Thy blood.

If faithful souls be alike glorified
As angels, then my father's soul doth see,
And adds this even to full felicity,
That valiantly I hell's wide mouth o'erstride.
But if our minds to these souls be descried
By circumstances, and by signs that be
Apparent in us not immediately,
How shall my mind's white truth by them be tried?
They see idolatrous lovers weep and mourn,
And vile blasphemous conjurers to call
On Jesu's name, and pharisaical
Dissemblers feign devotion. Then turn,
O pensive soul, to God, for He knows best
Thy grief, for He put it into my breast.

If poisonous minerals, and if that tree
Whose fruit threw death on—else immortal—us,
If lecherous goats, if serpents envious
Cannot be damn'd, alas! why should I be?
Why should intent or reason, born in me,
Make sins, else equal, in me more heinous?
And, mercy being easy, and glorious
To God, in His stern wrath why threatens He?
But who am I, that dare dispute with Thee?
O God, O! of Thine only worthy blood,
And my tears, make a heavenly Lethean flood,
And drown in it my sins' black memory.
That Thou remember them, some claim as debt;
I think it mercy if Thou wilt forget.

Death be not proud, though some have callèd thee
Mighty and dreadful, for, thou art not so,
For those whom thou think'st thou dost overthrow
Die not, poor Death, nor yet canst thou kill me.
From rest and sleep, which but thy pictures be,
Much pleasure, then from thee, much more must flow,
And soonest our best men with thee do go,
Rest of their bones, and souls' delivery.
Thou art slave to Fate, Chance, kings, and desperate men,
And dost with poison, war, and sickness dwell,
And poppy or charms can make us sleep as well
And better than thy stroke; why swell'st thou then?
One short sleep past, we wake eternally,
And death shall be no more; Death, thou shalt die.

Spit in my face, you Jews, and pierce my side,
Buffet, and scoff, scourge, and crucify me,
For I have sinn'd, and sin, and only He,
Who could do no iniquity, hath died.
But by my death can not be satisfied
My sins, which pass the Jews' impiety.
They kill'd once an inglorious man, but I
Crucify him daily, being now glorified.
O let me then His strange love still admire;
Kings pardon, but He bore our punishment;
And Jacob came clothed in vile harsh attire,
But to supplant, and with gainful intent;
God clothed Himself in vile man's flesh, that so
He might be weak enough to suffer woe.

Why are we by all creatures waited on?
Why do the prodigal elements supply
Life and food to me, being more pure than I,
Simpler and further from corruption?
Why brook'st thou, ignorant horse, subjection?
Why dost thou, bull and boar, so sillily
Dissemble weakness, and by one man's stroke die,
Whose whole kind you might swallow and feed upon?
Weaker I am, woe's me, and worse than you;
You have not sinn'd, nor need be timorous.
But wonder at a greater, for to us
Created nature doth these things subdue;
But their Creator, whom sin, nor nature tied,
For us, His creatures, and His foes, hath died.

What if this present were the world's last night?
Mark in my heart, O soul, where thou dost dwell,
The picture of Christ crucified, and tell
Whether His countenance can thee affright.
Tears in His eyes quench the amazing light;
Blood fills his frowns, which from His pierced head fell;
And can that tongue adjudge thee unto hell,
Which pray'd forgiveness for His foes' fierce spite?
No, no; but as in my idolatry
I said to all my profane mistresses,
Beauty of pity, foulness only is
A sign of rigour; so I say to thee,
To wicked spirits are horrid shapes assign'd;
This beauteous form assures a piteous mind.

Batter my heart, three-person'd God, for you
As yet but knock; breathe, shine, and seek to mend;
That I may rise and stand, o'erthrow me, and bend
Your force to break, blow, burn, and make me new.
I, like an usurp'd town, to another due,
Labour to admit you, but O, to no end.
Reason, your viceroy in me, me should defend,
But is captiv'd, and proves weak or untrue.
Yet dearly I love you, and would be lov'd fain,
But am betroth'd unto your enemy;
Divorce me, untie, or break that knot again,
Take me to you, imprison me, for I
Except you enthrall me, never shall be free,
Nor ever chaste, except you ravish me.

Wilt thou love God as he thee? then digest,
My soul, this wholesome meditation,
How God the Spirit, by angels waited on
In heaven, doth make His temple in thy breast.
The Father having begot a Son most blest,
And still begetting—for he ne'er begun—
Hath deign'd to choose thee by adoption,
Co-heir to His glory, and Sabbath' endless rest.
And as a robb'd man, which by search doth find
His stolen stuff sold, must lose or buy it again,
The Sun of glory came down, and was slain,
Us whom He had made, and Satan stole, to unbind.
'Twas much, that man was made like God before,
But, that God should be made like man, much more.

Father, part of His double interest
Unto Thy kingdom Thy Son gives to me;
His jointure in the knotty Trinity
He keeps, and gives to me his death's conquest.
This Lamb, whose death with life the world hath blest,
Was from the world's beginning slain, and He
Hath made two wills, which with the legacy
Of His and Thy kingdom do thy sons invest.
Yet such are these laws, that men argue yet
Whether a man those statutes can fulfil.
None doth; but thy all-healing grace and Spirit
Revive again what law and letter kill.
Thy law's abridgement, and Thy last command
Is all but love; O let this last Will stand!

Since she whom I loved hath paid her last debt
To Nature, and to hers, and my good is dead,
And her soul early into heaven ravishèd,
Wholly on heavenly things my mind is set.
Here the admiring her my mind did whet
To seek thee, God; so streams do show the head;
But though I have found thee, and thou my thirst hast fed,
A holy thirsty dropsy melts me yet.
But why should I beg more love, whenas thou
Dost woo my soul, for hers offering all thine:
And dost not only fear lest I allow
My love to saints and angels, things divine,
But in thy tender jealousy dost doubt
Lest the world, flesh, yea, devil put thee out.

⌒

Show me, dear Christ, Thy spouse so bright and clear.
What! is it she which on the other shore
Goes richly painted? or which, robbed and tore,
Laments and mourns in Germany and here?
Sleeps she a thousand, then peeps up one year?
Is she self-truth, and errs? now new, now outwore?
Doth she, and did she, and shall she evermore
On one, on seven, or on no hill appear?
Dwells she with us, or like adventuring knights
First travel we to seek, and then make love?
Betray, kind husband, Thy spouse to our sights,
And let mine amorous soul court Thy mild dove,
Who is most true and pleasing to Thee then
When she is embraced and open to most men.

Oh, to vex me, contraries meet in one:
Inconstancy unnaturally hath begot
A constant habit; that when I would not
I change in vows, and in devotion.
As humorous is my contrition
As my profane love, and as soon forgot:
As riddlingly distempered, cold and hot,
As praying, as mute; as infinite, as none.
I durst not view heaven yesterday; and today
In prayers and flattering speeches I court God:
Tomorrow I quake with true fear of His rod.
So my devout fits come and go away
Like a fantastic ague; save that here
Those are my best days, when I shake with fear.

INDEX OF FIRST LINES